THE HUFFINGTON POST

COMPLETE GUIDE TO

BLOGGING

SIMON & SCHUSTER PAPERBACKS

New York   London   Toronto   Sydney

Simon & Schuster Paperbacks
A Division of Simon & Schuster, Inc.
1230 Avenue of the Americas
New York, NY 10020

First Simon & Schuster trade paperback edition December 2008

SIMON & SCHUSTER PAPERBACKS and colophon
are registered trademarks of Simon & Schuster, Inc.

For information about special discounts for bulk purchases,
please contact Simon & Schuster Special Sales at
1-800-456-6798 or business@simonandschuster.com.

Designed by Chris Welch

Manufactured in the United States of America

7   9   10   8   6

Library of Congress Cataloging-in-Publication Data
The Huffington Post complete guide to blogging / the editors of the Huffington Post ;
introduction by Arianna Huffington ; foreword by Kenneth Lerer.
p.   cm.
1. Blogs. 2. Blogs—Design. 3. Blogs—Management. I. Huffington post.
TK5105.8884.H86   2008
006.7—dc22   2008036520

ISBN 13: 978-1-4391-0500-9
ISBN 10:   1-4391-0500-6

CONTENTS

Part I
THE NUTS AND BOLTS OF BLOGGING

Part II
THE BLOG REVOLUTION IS HERE! BE A PART OF IT.

Part III
THE HUFFINGTON POST RESOURCE SECTION

FOREWORD

When I retired, Norman Lear gave me some crucial advice. Set up an office, keep in touch with people, stay in the flow as much or as little as you want. Things that interest you will cross your desk. And when they do, run with them.

I'd just launched an anti-NRA website, was spectacularly frustrated with the '04 elections, and had watched how well the Republican campaign used the Internet. My introduction to Arianna couldn't have come at a better time.

My favorite sport is baseball. And my favorite baseball book is *Moneyball: The Art of Winning an Unfair Game* by sportswriter Michael Lewis. My favorite quote from the book is:

> At the bottom of the Oakland experiment was a willingness to re-think baseball: how it is managed, how it is played, who is best suited to play it, and why. In what amounted to a systematic scientific investigation of their sport, the Oakland front office had re-examined everything from the market price of foot

speed, to the inherent difference between the average major-league player and the superior triple-A one.

It highlights perfectly Billy Beane's successful strategy as general manager of the Oakland A's during a time when baseball clubs were basically buying their wins with colossal budgets to spend on the best players in the league. How could he compete with the New York Yankees when he had a quarter of the money? He couldn't beat them at their own game. So he had to reinvent it, make it different, make it better, make it his own.

So when Arianna and I decided to start The Huffington Post, we were the Oakland A's of news sources. And we had to figure out a way to create a competitive media company without any of the preexisting resources. Our lack of a legacy was both an obstacle and a boon. On the one hand, we had no infrastructure, no team of reporters, no brand. On the other, we had no baggage—unlike a television network, or a print newspaper, or a magazine that has to reconfigure and translate itself into a new online medium. We were under no burden of a long-standing business model—we were free to create a brand-new one. Every penny we spent could go directly to our single focus. So while we had to overcome the fact that we were starting from nothing, we also had the benefit of starting from nothing.

With none of the traditional assets, we had to do it differently. There was no team of reporters, so we decided to aggregate news. What we *did* have was Arianna's unique Rolodex and a team that included the two of us and two extremely talented people: Jonah Peretti and Roy Sekoff. We also started one of the first group blogs. That simple combination of news and blog worked incredibly well, and it's one of the unique components that make us what we are. Nothing fancy, but it all made sense and created a spark—not only in our readers, but in us.

As hokey as it sounds, The Huffington Post really did start as a labor of love. And passion. And ideals. We wanted to be heard, to create a voice. We made something new because we strongly felt that it needed to exist, not because we thought it would make money. So we built it differently, like Billy Beane, and it all played out like Norman Lear said it would.

Never did I think HuffPost would become what it is today. Our initial, modest noise that began with a single page is now an ever-evolving, multilayered Internet newspaper. We've gone from aggregated news and politics-minded blogs to a source for obsessive coverage of everything from entertainment to the environment to business to fashion. And now we've also expanded geographically, becoming both a national voice and a local community.

Watching it all grow and develop has been enormously gratifying. And one of the key elements of our success has been our understanding of the importance of content and how to move it. Fast. And far. We're at the intersection of content and technology. It's what has allowed us to not only cover everything that reaches a tipping point, but also to help create tipping points with our coverage.

I think working in an online medium is a little like painting in oil—you try out a shade of green, and if you don't like it, you just paint right over it and make it blue. Or orange. Or whatever. Everything on the Internet is instant, up-to-the-minute, constantly changing and rearranging.

We've got a lot invested in the future. We've gone from a team of four to fifty. And our average age is twenty-eight—that is, if you take me and Arianna out of the mix. It's part of what makes us dynamic and unique.

As we continue to grow in the present, we have to stay focused on the bigger picture. When you're talking about the Internet, long-term can be awfully quick. But I'd like to hope that eventually, or maybe not so eventually, if you've got something to say, you'll want to say it on The Huffington Post.

Kenneth Lerer

INTRODUCTION

Bringing together people from different parts of my life and facilitating interesting conversations has always been part of my Greek DNA and upbringing. These conversations have taken place around dinner tables, or at book parties, or on hikes with groups of friends. With The Huffington Post, the idea was to take those conversations—about politics and books and art and music and food and sex—and bring them into cyberspace, creating a one-stop site for news and opinion with an attitude, in real time.

Although I had dabbled in the online world since 1998, with a website highlighting my books, newspaper columns, and various political crusades (including saying no to pollsters and pushing America to lessen its dependence on foreign oil), I really became addicted to the fast-moving blogosphere in 2002, on the heels of the Trent Lott/Strom Thurmond story. At a celebration for Thurmond's one hundredth birthday, Lott had declared that America would be better off had Thurmond—and presumably his segregationist views—carried the day decades earlier. Despite the outrageousness of the statement, the mainstream media completely dropped the ball on the story, all but ignoring it. Bloggers were the ones who ran with it and helped turn the smug Senate majority leader into the penitent *former* Senate majority leader, a clump of bloody political chum floating in a tank of hungry sharks. They proved you could move mountains—and take down a powerful leader—if you had an Internet connection, had your facts right, and were willing to go beyond the conventional wisdom.

The more I thought about it, the more it struck me that while so many of the most interesting things happening in our culture were happening online, many of the most interesting people I knew were not taking part.

Let's face it: It isn't easy maintaining a high-profile blog. You've got to be constantly churning out material. We now have a 24/7 news cycle—a beast that constantly needs to be fed. Creating a mega-sized group blog seemed like a natural solution. By having so many interesting people taking part, there would always be people posting things worth reading—even if some of our bloggers could post only every now and then. This allowed people who had a lot of compelling things to say—but not always enough time to say them—to blog without having to give up their day jobs.

It didn't hurt that HuffPost was created in the midst of a perfect storm for a political news and opinion site. Blogging was rapidly transforming the media structure in America. Twenty years ago, it took twenty years to build a new media brand. Ten years ago, it took ten. By 2005, we felt we could build a new media brand in a year. The Internet had flattened America's hierarchal media structure. You could get from point A to point B much, much quicker. You could reach the tipping point on a story or an issue sometimes overnight.

In the months leading to the launch of HuffPost, I always knew that I wanted our group blog to incorporate the best of the Old Media and the best of the New Media. And there was nobody better as a representative of the old establishment culture than Arthur Schlesinger Jr.

So the very first person I approached about blogging for Huff-Post was Arthur.

He invited me to lunch at the venerable Century Club to discuss it. I arrived to find Arthur and his wonderful wife, Alexandra, already seated at the table.

"What is a blog?" he asked. "And what is blogging?"

So in this bastion of the Old Guard, I found myself explaining to a man who didn't do e-mail, and who considered his fax machine a revolutionary way to communicate, what blogging is. Of course, he got it instantly—and almost as quickly agreed. With one proviso: "Can I fax you my blogs?" he said.

"Of course," I replied, since I've never agreed with the purists who say that it ain't blogging if it's not done on Movable Type.

And, indeed, his first faxed blog post arrived—and was posted—on May 9, 2005, the day HuffPost launched. On that day, President Bush had derided the Yalta conference as "one of the greatest wrongs of history"—part and parcel of his ongoing derision of negotiations, diplomacy, and anything but unilateral cowboyism.

And now here was Schlesinger, an expert on Yalta, swiftly and knowledgeably countering Bush's comment. It was my dream come true.

I am frequently asked if the rise of New Media is the death knell for Old Media. My answer is that Old Media isn't dead; it's critically ill but will actually be saved by the transfusion of passion and immediacy the New Media revolution has inspired. Blogging and the new media are transforming the way news and information are disseminated—serving as a wake-up call. A wake-up call the traditional media—after years of hitting the snooze button—has finally heeded. But it took a while.

I remember being on a panel around the time of the Lott affair organized by the Hollywood Radio and Television Society. It was filled with a number of familiar talking heads, including Larry King and Sam Donaldson. We were discussing the good, the bad, and the ugly of mainstream journalism. At one point I launched into a rant about all the important stories I felt were not getting the attention they deserved from the big media outlets.

My fellow panelists, on cue, leapt to the defense of their mainstream brethren, pointing out that many of the stories I mentioned had, in fact, been covered on TV or in the big daily papers.

And indeed they had. Sometimes in ninety-second news packages and sometimes even on the front page of *The New York Times*—above the fold.

But that, until the rise of the bloggers, was that. Issue noted. Let's all move on. Meaning, no follow-up, even as more details would come up. For too long, reporters for the big media outlets have been fixated on novelty, always moving all too quickly on to the next big score or the next hot get.

The problem wasn't that important stories weren't being covered. It was that they weren't being covered in the obsessive way that breaks through the din of our multimedia universe.

Paradoxically, in these days of instant communication and twenty-four-hour news cycles, it's actually easier to miss information we might otherwise pay attention to. That's why we need stories to be covered and re-covered and re-re-covered and covered again—until they become part of the cultural bloodstream.

The vast majority of mainstream journalists head in the direction the assignment desk points them. This often means following a candidate around, or sitting in the White House pressroom, and then rehashing the day's schedule for their readers or viewers.

That's why we see so many stories focusing on endless horse race "analysis" and tracking the results of the latest polls. Quoting polling data is now synonymous with reporting at many news organizations.

In biblical times, Jonah was condemned to a dark journey in the belly of the whale for his complacency and relentless triviality. Today, thanks to the mainstream media's complacency and relentless triviality, the American people have been condemned to the endlessly repeated bleating of the denizens of the media establishment echo chamber.

In contrast, bloggers are armed with a far more effective piece of access than a White House press credential: passion.

When bloggers decide that something matters, they chomp down hard and refuse to let go. They're the true pit bulls of reporting. The only way to get them off a story is to cut off their heads (and even then you'll need to pry their jaws open). And although many bloggers work alone, it's their collective effort that makes them so effective. They share information freely, feed off one another's work, argue with each other, and keep adding to the story.

And because blogs are constantly updated, bloggers will often start with a small story, or a piece of one—a contradictory quote, an unearthed document, a detail that doesn't add up—that the big outlets would deem too minor. But it's only minor until, well, it's not.

That kind of relentlessness was never available to me as a newspaper columnist. When I started blogging about Judy Miller and

The New York Times in 2005, it was something I never could have done as a columnist. My editors would have said, "Oh, you wrote about her last month."

Then there is the open nature of the form—the links, the research made visible, the democratic back and forth, the open archives, the big professorial messiness of it all. It reminds me of my schoolgirl days when providing the right answer wasn't enough for our teachers—they demanded that we "show our work." Bloggers definitely show their work. It's why you don't just read blogs—you experience them.

As someone who had spent her adult life toiling in the world of books and syndicated newspaper column-writing, where the eternal verities of beginning/middle/end are the Rosetta stone of structure, it was utterly liberating to find a place where the random thought is honored. Where a zippy one-off is enough to spark a flurry of impassioned replies. And where reaching the climax too quickly is okay.

Blogs are by nature very personal—an intimate, often ferocious expression of the blogger's passions. You're much more intimate when you're writing a blog than when you're writing a column, let alone a book—it's the conversational nature of it, the way that it draws people in and includes them in the dialogue. You may set out to write about politics, but in the end, you write about yourself, about the things you care about beyond politics. And this creates a close bond between blogger and audience.

It really does become a conversation. Before I started blogging, I'd have an idea on a Monday, write a column about it on Tuesday, it would be published on Wednesday . . . and readers would respond with letters to the editor two or three days later. Now, I can get an idea Monday morning, blog about it, and immediately get comments. And these comments then take on a life of their own, as HuffPost's community of commenters begins responding to me and to each other.

One of the defining moments for New Media came soon after our launch—in July 2005, to be precise, with the London bombings. I was having my morning coffee and reading my paper copy of *The New York Times,* which had a front-page photo of Londoners celebrating their city winning its bid to host the 2012 Olympics—literally yesterday's news. In the meantime, HuffPost not only had the bombings as our news splash but HuffPost's London-based bloggers weighing in with real-time reactions.

The tech advances of the last few years have turned the news and entertainment worlds on their ears, shifting the balance of power away from media pooh-bahs dictating what is important and what is not, and toward consumers—and citizens—being empowered to choose and create.

Technology is having the same game-changing effect on the political world—as well as on those assigned to cover it.

The 2008 campaign has been the first truly twenty-first-century presidential race. We have entered the era where candidates routinely announce their candidacy, try out and place campaign ads, and raise hundreds of millions of dollars online. And they are connecting to voters via increasingly interactive websites.

By going online, campaigns are able to engage a whole new generation of young voters who spend so much of their time—and get so much of their information—online. It's where they get their news; it's where they share their views (and their pictures, videos, favorite songs, diaries, and more). It's how they stay connected to their friends—and how they can become connected to the candidates. Politics and technology are intersecting like never before.

And yet, a quick survey of the way much of the '08 race was covered by the mainstream media is like being stuck in a time warp. Sure, many newspapers have added blogs and interactive widgets aggregating their coverage, but the follow-the-candidates'-planes-and-take-down-the-nuggets-of-spun-wisdom-doled-out-by-campaign-spokesmen model is still very much in effect. In a time of broadband politics, many in the traditional media are still adjusting their rabbit ears.

As a result, blogging has been the greatest breakthrough in popular journalism since Tom Paine—and the blogosphere is the most vital news source in our country.

And it's why I am so excited about this book.

Our team of editors—helped along by contributions from some of HuffPost's top bloggers—really has succeeded in putting together, as the title says, a complete guide to blogging. In it, you'll find tools to build your blog, strategies to create your community, tips on finding your voice, and entertaining anecdotes that will make you wonder what took you so long to start blogging in the first place. Whether you are a total newcomer trying to figure out what all the fuss is about, or an old pro looking for ways to help get your blog noticed, this book will provide a fun, easy-to-use, and valuable resource.

Time to get started. Your bloggy future awaits. Come on in . . . the water and the blogging are fine.

Arianna Huffington

PART I

THE NUTS AND BOLTS OF BLOGGING

CHAPTER 1

WELCOME TO THE WORLD OF BLOGS

*Blogging is the only addiction that won't make you fat,
drunk or stoned. But it might make you so hungry for
instant gratification that your books get shorter.*
—Erica Jong, novelist, *HuffPost blogger*

Yes, yes, we get the irony. We're writing a *book* about blogs. Where is the comments section? Where are the links? By the time you're thumbing through this at the bookstore several months will have transpired since we wrote these words. With no comments from readers. Or updates.

But believe it or not, a book about blogging fits neatly into this juncture in communication history. You see, printed books themselves were once a rather revolutionary idea. Six hundred years ago, if people wanted to share ideas, they had few options. We could shout our complaints from the barn rafters. Maybe a few chickens would hear us. We could scrawl or draw our musings and post them in the town square—but soon the elements would take their toll. Documents were preserved, of course—medieval monks specialized in hand-copying important texts—but to justify years of a monk's time, these documents had to be privileged indeed. Few normal people could spare five years to hand-write their stories.

Then, in mid-fifteenth-century Germany, printer Johannes Gutenberg happened upon a discovery: By creating type pieces out of metal—known as movable type—and arranging them to form words, you could make multiple copies of a document far faster than a monk could write. Gutenberg's most famous creation was the Gutenberg Bible, but before long, people were using movable type to print science books, political commentaries, and other works that fundamentally changed the world.

Fast-forward to 2001. Somewhere in California, a twentysomething woman named Mena Trott, laid off from her dot-com job, started keeping an online diary of her life. She called it Dollar Short (as in a day late and a . . .). She wasn't happy with the available online publishing tools. So she and her husband, Ben, decided to create their own. On October 8, 2001, they released their contribution to the nascent blogging software industry. You could download it free of charge (though donations to the Trott rent fund were certainly welcome). With a wink at the past, they called the software Movable Type.

So there you have the blog/book connection: from movable type, to books, to books *on* Movable Type. Is blogging as big a revolution as what Gutenberg started? Only time will tell. But since we at The Huffington Post like to report on news and history in the making, we'd like to help you, dear reader, get started on making some history of your own.

What Is a Blog?

A blog at its most fundamental level is simply a "web log." That is, a regularly updated account of events or ideas posted on the web.

But calling blogs mere updated web diaries is a bit like calling poetry a pleasant arrangement of words on a page. There is an art to this. Those of us who work at HuffPost believe we are fortunate enough to be present at the advent of a new form of human communication—one that is more interactive, more democratic, and just more fun than what has come before.

Blogs can bring down a Senate majority leader. They can show what a presidential candidate talks about in unguarded moments. They can provide stay-at-home parents with a little space to rant about the tragedy of colic (or maybe share updates on a local environmental issue—and Brad Pitt—during naps). They cut out the gatekeepers of information and shorten the news cycle. They give companies new ways to communicate with customers and shareholders—and give customers and shareholders new ways to make their voices heard. Blogging gives you a feeling of satisfaction that writing a letter to the editor, or a letter to the "customer care" department of a corporation, cannot match. The public nature of blogs means that any of the billion people on this planet who own or have access to a computer can read what any of the rest of us is saying. That's true even if what we're saying is about a niche (for instance, issues germane to the mini off-road buggy community) that in the past would have gotten us labeled as freaks. In fact, because the potential audience is so huge, there is space for just about every topic you can imagine. As we link to each other, the marketplace of ideas sorts out who is worth listening to and who is not. A congressman's statement on an issue does not necessarily take precedence over a constituent's, the way it often does in a traditional news story.

It is this mix of the high and low, the personal and the political, that makes blogs so fascinating and so important in an open society. When we launched HuffPost in 2005, we knew we liked blogs, but even we underestimated how head over heels we'd fall. "Blogging is definitely the most interesting thing I've done as a writer, and I've been writing full-time since the late seventies," Carol Felsenthal, author of *Clinton in Exile: A President Out of the White House* and a HuffPost blogger, tells us. "I used to walk my dog, Henry, first thing in the morning. Now I'm often at my computer writing a post while Henry looks at me and wonders what happened to the good old days when his owner was compulsive but not hyper-compulsive."

It's the informality and the immediacy that make blogging addictive for many of us. No editor stands between us and the public. This leads to a lot of rumors and other fluff going up on the web. But it's also enormously liberating. You can put all kinds of ideas out there. "My thoughts don't all have to be fully baked," says Marci Alboher, who writes the "Shifting Careers" column and blog for *The New York Times.* She posts an idea and sees what her readers think. "They help me solve the problem and let me know if I'm going down the right path. It helps me figure out what the issues are very quickly."

It is this multidirectional conversation—giving all of us a platform, expanding the scope of news, and making it a shared enterprise between producers and consumers—that makes blogs so revolutionary. We have a lot of fun blogging. We're writing this book because we're pretty sure you will too.

The History of Blogs

For all that blogging is changing society, it's important to remember just how new it is. Remember Elián González, the Cuban boy that the entire country was obsessed with in the spring of 2000? His story had the markings of a blogosphere sensation: memorable photos, passionate opinions on U.S./Cuban policy, a political hot potato for the Clinton administration. But it was only a mainstream media mainstay because the blogosphere as we know it today had not yet evolved. The linking, commenting, and annotating we find commonplace today was still to come.

The term "weblog" was coined in 1997 by Jorn Barger, the editor of Robot Wisdom (itself a blog, albeit one with some nasty anti-Semitism bopping around on it, so we don't recommend you humor him by visiting the site). The shortened word "blog" was coined by Adaptive Path founder and former Epinions.com creative director Peter Merholz on his website (peterme.com) in 1999.

The number of blogs was small at first. According to Technorati (a company that conducts a sort of blogging census), the one millionth blog came online in the fall of 2003. At that time, people were creating blogs at a rate of about five thousand to six thousand per day. But the rate soon picked up. The blog total hit four million in the fall of 2004, around the time that blogs really exploded on the national radar screen for their role in the flap about memos related to President Bush's National Guard service. By that time, twelve thousand new blogs were coming online each day. Like a colony of bacteria, the blogosphere continued to post a quick doubling rate through 2005 (fourteen million blogs in August) and 2006 (fifty-seven million blogs in October). These days, Technorati is tracking 112 million blogs. Web users create approximately fifty thousand new blogs a day. This being the web, about three to seven thousand of these new blogs are nothing but spam, spam, and links to more spam. The rate of doubling has slowed as the blogosphere has matured. But new voices are still coming online in droves.

The demographics of the blogosphere could be the subject of several blog posts in their own right. For instance, in late 2006, the most common language for blogs was actually not English.

Q&A with Peter Merholz, the "Blog Father"

HUFFPOST: Why did you start blogging (before it was called that)?

MERHOLZ: I started blogging because I wanted to make a name for myself. In 1998, I was a neophyte interaction designer with a lot of ideas. I wanted to get known for my ideas, and, having been a web developer for the prior few years, I had no fear of posting things online. At the job I had at the time, I was known as the guy who sent interesting URLs around on internal mailing lists, and I realized that there was likely a broader audience who would appreciate my efforts.

HUFFPOST: How did you think up the word "blog"?

MERHOLZ: There was a word, "weblog," used to describe the kind of site I was maintaining, with lists of links and annotations of the web. I shifted the syllables from web-log to we-blog, and that became "blog."

HUFFPOST: Were you surprised how quickly it caught on?

MERHOLZ: Yes. It benefited from the rise of the tool "Blogger," the first popular technology for maintaining blogs.

HUFFPOST: Do you ever get any special treatment for having coined such a popular word?

MERHOLZ: I've been interviewed for TV and radio [such as NPR's *Morning Edition*] because of it, and it's a great conversation starter, particularly with lexicographers.

According to Technorati, it was Japanese (37 percent). English (at the time) was a close second at 36 percent. About 8 percent of blog posts are in Chinese and 1 percent is written in Farsi (the language spoken in Iran and some of the former Soviet republics). According to a 2006 survey from the Pew Internet and American Life Project, more than half of American bloggers (54 percent) are under age thirty. Both men and women blog at equal rates, but bloggers are less likely to be white (60 percent) than other

Internet users (74 percent) and more likely to be Hispanic (19 percent vs. 11 percent).

The majority of the 112 million blogs out there will never grab more than a few readers. That's OK; 37 percent of bloggers told the Pew survey that keeping in touch with friends and family was a major reason for blogging, and 52 percent said they blogged mostly for themselves rather than for an audience. On the other hand, the most popular blogs—Boing Boing, Engadget, Gizmodo, TechCrunch, and HuffPost—get millions of unique visitors every month.

To Blog or Not to Blog: Top Ten Reasons Why You Should

1. To build a reputation as a wise, thoughtful expert on family values.

2. To destroy someone else's reputation as a wise, thoughtful expert on family values with one drunken photo from the all-nude male cabaret.

3. To entertain the fantasy that a baby-model scout is looking at photos of your child in a too-cute Burberry two-piece toddler swimsuit ($55).

4. Pure exhibitionism.

5. To vent about your halitosis-plagued boss and boneheaded corporate policies.

6. To establish cred for a new career after being fired by your halitosis-plagued boss and bone-headed HR minions.

7. To let the world know that your babysitter is trying to extort $1.5 million from you.

8. To stop a rumor that you sexually harassed said babysitter.

9. Grandma gently suggests that you share your rants about (pick one) the 2000 election, Mumia Abu-Jamal, the need for a border fence, or the "Klintoons" with someone other than her.

10. For the opportunity to make an additional $1.65 per week through Google AdWords or the Amazon Associates program.

Anytime you get lots of eyeballs in one place, there is money to be made. According to a 2008 report from the firm eMarketer, advertising spending on blogs reached $283 million in 2007. The company projected this would rise to $746 million in 2012. For comparison, companies, politicians, and others spend over $70 billion on TV advertising each year and $40 billion on newspaper advertising. We don't think these industries are going to disappear. Nonetheless, as mediums converge, and as online properties allow for better advertisement targeting, blogs offer one of the few revenue growth spots in the media world. Newspaper ad revenue fell 12 percent last year. Even the best newspapers are slashing newsroom jobs.

Why Blog?

I blog because I am.
—*Cali Williams Yost, Work + Life Fit blog,*
blogger for Fast Company

Why blog? Here's a better question: Why not blog? As you'll learn in the upcoming chapters, blogging is easier than smoking, can take less time and money, and isn't banned in restaurants. According to the 2006 Pew survey, 59 percent of active bloggers spend just one to two hours a week on their hobby. Unlike smoking, you can also quit whenever you want. Many people do just that. There may be 112 million blogs in the blogosphere, but only 7.4 million, Technorati tells us, have been updated in the last ninety days.

Fair enough, you say. But what do I write about? We'll cover this more in depth in chapter 2, "Getting Started," but in the meantime, here's some great advice from Penelope Trunk, a blogger and *Boston Globe* career columnist: "Pick a topic—you can

THE RIGHT NETSTUFF

HARRY SHEARER, WRITER, ACTOR, DIRECTOR, MUSICIAN, AND HUFFPOST BLOGGER

My career as a blogger actually began before the word was even invented. I had volunteered to cover the second, civil trial of O. J. Simpson for Slate.com, primarily because, unlike the criminal trial, this one would not be televised, and, having wasted so many hours on the first act of the drama, I couldn't bear to miss the grinding detail of the second, final act.

Slate gave me the one thing I needed: all the space I might want to use whenever I wanted to use it. My response was to write a daily dispatch from the courthouse, except for the days when nothing interesting transpired and the week I was in Australia. When I did write, I combined factual reportage of the trial's proceedings with what I imagined to be the musings of a guy sitting next to you in the courtroom, digging his elbow playfully into your side and whispering impolite observations about the way the participants looked and talked and strategized and blundered.

What I was doing, it turned out later, was blogging—joyfully mixing fact and opinion, writing or not writing as the spirit moved me, responsible, really, to no one but my readers. It was, as Jimmy Dean might have said, everything but the links.

When the trial ended, so did that project. And when weblogs started up a few years later, I didn't recognize the form. I viewed the development from afar with the slightly bored distance I now reserve for, let's say, Twitter.

But then I started reading blogs—Talking Points Memo, Instapundit, Kausfiles, Informed Comment, Little Green Footballs—realizing that their voraciousness in reading, absorbing, and reacting to the information and misinformation on the Net could vastly amplify my own ability to consume the great indigestible ball of Netstuff. When Arianna called, I was ready to enlist, and the rest, as they say, is toast. Or history. I forget what they say.

change it when you know what you're doing. This is like dating. Pick something that seems good, and if it isn't, try again. Don't get hung up on topic. As in dating, you'll know when you've found one that's the right fit. There are some obvious things, like pick a topic you have a lot to say about, pick something that interests you, pick something that will help your career. This is great advice, but you already know that if you look for a perfect match you'll never actually go on a date." Here's another reason to blog: Even if quit rates are high, with 2.13 million blog posts going up in the past seven days, chances are you know a lot of people who are blogging. Your colleagues may be blogging when they're "forgetting" to read your sales report. Your neighbors may be blogging instead of bringing in those unsightly trash cans from the curb. The old guy next door who spends a long time lingering at the window in his underwear? He's *definitely* blogging. Your children are blogging. In fact, they're probably blogging right now about your lame attempts to lose weight by drinking low-carb beer. We wouldn't rule out commentary from your spouse on your Cheez Whiz–for–breakfast habit either. So isn't it time you had your say?

More seriously, though, we find blogging to be a great opportunity for creative expression, whether you have many outlets or none at all. Nora Ephron—who has multiple ways of expressing herself through books, movies, columns, and the like—has said she loves the unique expression blogs allow. She's not the only ones who feels this way. According to the Pew survey, 52 percent of bloggers said that expressing themselves creatively was a major reason for blogging, and 54 percent said they had never published their writings or media creations elsewhere.

The main reason to blog is that you have something to say to the world—and you want to see what the world has to say back.

Why Do You Blog?

TO AVOID THE LOONY BIN

Bob Cesca, AUTHOR OF *ONE NATION UNDER FEAR*
AND HUFFPOST BLOGGER

"If I hadn't discovered blogging during the Bush years, I probably would be in a padded room somewhere. To that point, the most satisfying reason why I blog is that it's a form of catharsis—being able to respond to politicians and the corporate media without having to be employed by either, and while not necessarily having to walk a picket line."

TO FIGHT INJUSTICE

Leslie Goldman, AUTHOR OF *LOCKER ROOM DIARIES*
AND HUFFPOST BLOGGER

"A snarky blog I wrote for HuffPost about a female-only BA degree in homemaking [at Southwestern Baptist Theological Seminary] attracted a producer from CNN. The next thing I knew, I was squaring off, live, against the dean of the university. I'm a body image writer but the topic irked so many of my feminist notions that it didn't matter that my background wasn't in education or gender studies; my passion shined through and I took that dean *down*!"

AS A SUBSTITUTE FOR THERAPY

Bree Barton, DANTE, DEGREED BLOG, AND BLOGGER FOR
CAPE COD TODAY

"My blog was also a way for me to cope with the existential crisis of being a college graduate. Those first few months weren't pretty; I'm not sure I've ever felt so lost. The post-college world is a bit of a wasteland. Since I'd always been a school addict, graduating really threw me for a loop. My blog offered an opportunity to process my experiences by writing about them. I had excellent fodder for my first entry: I had just been to a temp agency, a truly horrifying experience and the quintessential post-commencement moment. Blogging allowed me a chance to reflect and see the humor in my angst. It also helped keep me sane when I very seriously considered gnawing my fingers off (or going to grad school, a close second)."

TO KNOW YOU'RE NOT ALONE

Jeremy Adam Smith, DADDY DIALECTIC BLOG

"When I became the primary caregiver for my son, I found it to be really emotionally challenging, and I wanted to write about that as a way of trying to understand how I was changing. I couldn't relate at all to the parenting magazines out there, but one day I did a Google search for 'stay at home dad' and discovered this world of dad blogs, as well as smart, progressive mom blogs. I saw my life reflected in those, and I learned a lot. It took about a week for me to realize that I could start my own blog without too much trouble.

"I tried to write when I got the time, in early-morning or late-night snatches. I discovered that blogging is really an ideal vehicle for writing when you're being constantly interrupted by a crying baby. My posts are still just a series of rough drafts; I think of the blog as a notebook. I've since turned many posts into magazine articles or integrated their ideas and information into my book [*Twenty-First-Century Dad: How Stay-at-Home Fathers (and Breadwinning Moms) are Transforming the American Family,* Beacon Press, spring 2009]. In the blog I try to be aggressive and adventurous and experimental. As a result, sometimes I am just wrong or offbeat, but I really try to listen to my readers' feedback. Some comments on the blog changed my ideas, or pointed me in new directions, or helped me to understand my life as a father better. I'm very grateful to my readers."

TO TAP THE CREATIVE INNER SPIRIT

Jamie Lee Curtis, ACTRESS AND HUFFPOST BLOGGER

"I like blogging. The first time I blogged, like the first time I wrote a book, I didn't know I was doing it. I was just expressing an idea, an idea that wasn't even formed until it made it on paper. No edit. No 'What does/will this mean?' Just an idea. The individual roving mind of a woman. My mind. Something had happened in the world, it had been presented in the press, and I had a very strong feeling about it. I like that a blog gives the blogger a chance at expression without a publishing deal or a marketing plan and an eleven-city tour. I like that it goes out *fast* and becomes part of a larger dialogue and discourse. I like how the comments go down their own paths, tangents being commented on that really have no relevance to the original idea, just the free, roving minds of a populace, churning out ideas and more ideas.

"John Steinbeck in *East of Eden* wrote:

Our species is the only creative species, and it has only one creative instrument, the individual mind and spirit of a man. Nothing was ever created by two men. There are no good collaborations, whether in music, in art, in poetry, in mathematics, in philosophy. Once the miracle of creation has taken place, the group can build and extend it, but the group never invents anything. The preciousness lies in the lonely mind of a man. And now the forces marshaled around the concept of the group have declared a war of extermination on that preciousness, the mind of man. By disparagement, by starvation, by repressions, forced direction, and the stunning hammerblows of con-

ditioning, the free, roving mind is being pursued, roped, blunted, drugged. It is a sad suicidal course our species seems to have taken. And this I believe: that the free, exploring mind of the individual human is the most valuable thing in the world. And this I would fight for: the freedom of the mind to take any direction it wishes, undirected. And this I must fight against: any idea, religion, or government which limits or destroys the individual. This is what I am and what I am about. I can understand why a system built on a pattern must try to destroy the free mind, for that is the one thing which can by inspection destroy such a system.

"I second that. That is what I think blogging does: allows the individual minds of men and women to explore the limitlessness of their vast potential. I think we as a species are on a suicidal course, wanting more, having more, feeding ourselves and our children on ephemeral pleasures and poisons. Blogging allows contrary ideas into the societal vein and maybe, just maybe these ideas will be absorbed by the next generations who are the ones that will have to make the change that we need to survive."

What This Book Will Cover

Blogging is like the game Othello: It takes a minute to learn and a lifetime to master. If you're a newbie, we hope this book will give you the confidence you need to get started, or to move your blog to "active" status. If you're an experienced blogger and want to blog better, we will show you how.

The first section shows you how to start. We start with a very basic question: What should your blog be about? Then we cover the technical side: different blog hosts (Blogger, TypePad, Live-

Journal, etc.) and the pros and cons of each. For the advanced set, we look at podcasting, video blogs (or "vlogs"), tumblelogs, and other variations on the theme.

Then we'll look at some blogging best practices. What kind of template works best? (Please, no black background and teal text. We're begging you.) How do you choose good titles? You can customize your posts with photos and other art items that will draw readers in. We'll teach you how to write a bio that intrigues people and makes them want to listen to you. We'll teach you how to create a blogroll—that is, links to other blogs that cover complementary topics and whose creators might also link to you. We'll complete this section with a primer on linking to other web pages within your blog posts, using pull quotes, and the ever-important ethical and legal question of what constitutes fair use of copyrighted materials.

Once you have a blog, you want the world to know about it. We'll cover how to measure traffic using Site Meter, StatCounter, or Google Analytics. We'll show you how to figure out if other bloggers are mentioning you and how to draw more readers in. You'll learn how to build buzz for your site with Yahoo! Buzz, Digg, Delicious, and other tools. We'll include tips from people who work in public relations and bloggers who have managed to get their musings mentioned in all sorts of media outlets.

If you'd like to try to make some money with your blog, be sure to check out the section on using Google AdSense, Amazon Associates, and Yahoo! Publisher Network, as well as some other blog business models.

After you've got the nuts and bolts down, it's time to master the form. In chapter 4, we'll talk about finding your voice. Don't worry if you didn't get the best grades in English class as a kid or if your term papers came home bleeding red ink. Anyone can learn to write better, and even good writers may need some help learning the tools and tricks of the blogging trade. In general, a good blogger has a strong voice, a unique writing style, and a passion for what she's covering. She knows her audience well and aims to be part of the conversation with other bloggers in her community. She goes where the mainstream media doesn't. We'll show you the difference between how the mainstream media might cover an event and how a blogger would.

A key difference between mainstream journalism and the blogosphere (the community of bloggers on the web) is that blogs are just that: a community. In chapter 5 we'll talk about building a community around your blog. At HuffPost, we're fortunate to have two-thousand-plus bloggers and millions of readers conversing, boisterously, around the clock. In the old days, when a newspaper arrived on your doorstep (and it still does for many of us here at HuffPost), if a columnist ticked you off, all you could do was yell, nutcase-style, at the editorial page. (OK, you could also line your birdcage with it. But the columnist didn't *know* you were doing this.) On HuffPost, our bloggers often check back multiple times a day to see what their readers think. They engage with them. This chapter will talk about how to encourage comments, how to take criticism, how to be a good member of the blog community, and how to deal with the occasional cranks whose inappropriate posts scare off other readers.

Over the last few years, HuffPost has learned a lot about breaking news and building a community. So in the second section of this book, we'll share our story and the stories of some other blogs that have reshaped the media (and communication more generally). We're proud to have been part of this revolution. You'll hear about blogging successes, such as how our own Mayhill Fowler

HOW BLOGGING UNITES VOICES

DAVID BROMWICH, PROFESSOR OF ENGLISH AT YALE AND HUFFPOST BLOGGER

I posted about the drift in American opinion toward a soft consensus for torture. A retired policewoman from Texas wrote to say that throughout her career she had treated prisoners within their rights, and it was a matter of civic pride with her to have worked in a country where such an assumption of innocence was the law, even in dealing with violent criminals. The demoralization of the official policy on torture was accordingly a shame that she felt deeply. A similar commentary came from a veteran of the Second World War who had fought in Okinawa. This seems to me a good reason for writing—to bring out the force of feelings of humanity that persist under the political culture of the Bush-Cheney years.

broke the story about Senator Barack Obama referring to small-town voters as "bitter."

Broadly, we believe that the cause of democracy is served by having more information out there. We believe that democracy is advanced by having more voices included in the conversation. When everyone is a journalist, everyone can serve the journalist's role of keeping watch on our leaders and sharing stories that outrage or inspire. Blogging also teaches us that we all have the power to determine what is news. For you, your child's first steps may be as much a part of your news as an election. People have talked a lot about blogs, but this fundamentally democratic aspect of them is just beginning to be understood.

We are also just beginning to understand how blogs can bring us together. In 2000, the sociologist Robert Putnam wrote a book about the decline of American community called *Bowling Alone: The Collapse and Revival of American Community*. He fretted that

Americans were no longer joining Rotary clubs and volunteer groups, or even having friends over for dinner. He worried that we were destroying our social capital and becoming increasingly lonely. But the truth is that communities haven't disappeared (something Putnam acknowledged by including Craigslist as an example of a modern-day civic society in his 2003 book *Better Together: Restoring the American Community*). They've just changed. Now, bowling enthusiasts can read blogs written by bowlers in different time zones and comment on someone's unanticipated fifteen-strike streak. They may never share a bowling alley, but they're creating social networks all the same. Furthermore, these social networks aren't as inhibited by our in-person tendencies to meet up with folks of the same race, gender, age, sexual orientation, and disability status. We judge fellow bloggers on their ideas and their wit. Personally, we think that's a much better way to choose compatriots for this raucous RSS (Really Simple Syndication—but more on that later) feed called life. And who knows, maybe someone you meet through blogging will turn out to be a face-to-face neighbor as well.

EXPECT THE UNEXPECTED

CHRISTINE WHELAN, AUTHOR OF *MARRY SMART: THE INTELLIGENT WOMAN'S GUIDE TO TRUE LOVE* AND HUFFPOST BLOGGER

I moved from New York City to Iowa City in 2006, and when the Iowa Caucus rolled around in January 2007, I knew I'd be there—and be blogging. I posted a blog the morning of the Iowa Caucus, expressing my New Yorker's trepidation about something so community-based as group voting. I was pleasantly surprised to see that it remained in the featured blog spot all day long. That night, I blogged about my misadventures at my caucus location: I'd ended up in the wrong room; I was publicly humiliated and nearly committed voter fraud. Plus, I was dressed in high heels and a gold puffer coat, looking about as out of place as possible on that frigid night in a small University Heights, Iowa, high school cafeteria.

I put the whole silly tale up on The Huffington Post at 11 P.M. that night, assuming I'd be roundly mocked by folks in far-flung states (and hopefully supported by displaced New Yorkers everywhere). Rather than tell the world who I voted for, I ended my blog with this:

> So who did I vote for? If you'd been there, you'd know, but since you weren't, I'll retain the little bit of privacy about my vote still afforded to me.
>
> And if you were one of those 450 people who saw a girl in a gold puffer coat dash out the door of your high school auditorium precinct tonight, it's great to meet you. Yeah, I'm the new girl, from New York.

The next morning, I logged in to see the comments. The second one was from JoePolitico:

> I was in your group last night. I'll keep it a secret too. Welcome to UH.

I used to think blogging was sort of anonymous. Sure, people read what you write, but no one you *know*, and certainly not someone you've never met who *saw you* at the scene of the blog. So I've spent the last six months trying to figure out who JoePolitico is . . . and when I do, his secret will be safe with me, too.

"SOAP BUBBLES"

NORA EPHRON, AUTHOR, FILMMAKER, AND HUFFPOST BLOGGER

When I first started blogging, I didn't understand anything at all about it. I thought a blog was like other short things, like essays for instance, which are polished and have a kind of history as to form and structure. I made the mistake of reading the comments on my first few blogs, and my feelings were hurt. And I was astonished that my blogs, whether they were good or bad, vanished after 24 hours. I was once in daily journalism, and I am not unused to publishing things that last for only a day, but for many years I've been writing for magazines and books, and it seemed to me shocking and tragic that my immortal words were anything but.

But then I saw. In fact, you might almost say the shades fell from my eyes. Blogs were different from whatever had gone before. They weren't meant to be polished, like essays. They were informal, they were temporal. The comments they engendered weren't comments at all, although they were logged and enumerated as comments; they were instead a conversation, and one of the reasons for blogging was to start the conversation and to create the community that comes together briefly to talk about things they might not be talking about if you hadn't written your blog. The short lifespan wasn't a detriment, it was the point: A blog was a soap bubble, meant to last just a moment or two. The medium is the message: The medium was high-speed and the message appeared quickly and vanished just as quickly. The odds on a blog being relevant or even comprehensible days later were remote; just as well that it lasted only a moment.

And a blog didn't have to end, as essays do. It simply had to stop.

CHAPTER 2

GETTING STARTED

Like moving to a new home, starting a blog is always an adventure. This chapter shows you how to choose your spot of real estate in the blogosphere, hang the curtains, and arrange the furniture.

Every blogger starts by asking herself two main questions:

- What do I want to write about?
- How do I go about doing that?

The first part of this chapter will look at the first question—how to choose a topic that, broadly, will keep you interested long enough that you'll give your blog a decent go. Plenty of people blog under their own names, but if you want a snazzy title or nom de blog, we'll look at how to pull that off (and the downsides of pseudonyms).

The second part of the chapter will deal with the technical side of blogging. We'll talk about the different blog hosts and the physical process of putting a blog together. Blogging has its own conventions of design and etiquette that considerate bloggers make sure to know. We'll diagram a blog post and also talk a little bit about fair use and copyright, which—despite what some people think—do still exist on the Internet.

A STAR IS BORN

Q&A WITH DYLAN LOEWE, FORMER EXECUTIVE DIRECTOR OF BATTLEGROUND, COLUMBIA LAW STUDENT, AND HUFFPOST BLOGGER

HUFFPOST: How did you get started blogging?

LOEWE: Shortly after Super Tuesday [2008], I began getting a number of calls from friends and family asking me questions like "Is it over for Obama?" and "What's a superdelegate?" To make things easier, I wrote up a lengthy explanation of everything they needed to know about the election to that point and why, despite the chatter in the mainstream media, Obama was well positioned to win the nomination. I e-mailed it to about twenty people, one of whom suggested I stick it on a blog. So I did that and, on a whim, e-mailed the post to Ben Smith at Politico. He linked to it on his site, which led to Noam Scheiber of *The New Republic* linking to it on his site. Four days later, I was invited to write for The Huffington Post. One week after that, [UK newspaper] *The Guardian* invited me to be a weekly op-ed contributor. It was like living through a poorly written movie script.

HUFFPOST: Tell us your favorite story about blogging.

LOEWE: I once wrote a blog post for The Huffington Post that was posted in the top slot on the front page. When they stuck me in that spot, it meant Harry Reid got bumped down into the slot beneath me. Shortly thereafter, Hillary Clinton posted on the site, knocking me out of my spot. There I was, sandwiched between Hillary Clinton and Harry Reid, wondering if I'd somehow been mistaken for someone important.

What Do I Want to Write About?

It's perfectly fine to write about your life and experiences. That's the top reason bloggers give for starting a blog—and there's no need to apologize for it. As the second-wave feminists liked to say, the personal is political. Your grief at paying $4 a gallon for gasoline, your struggle to combine work and family, your happiness at hearing good news from a high school friend who's serving in Iraq—all are relevant to the world's ongoing conversation.

Even if there's no clear connection to larger events, don't fret about it. The great thing about the web is that it frees us from the tyranny of space and airtime that has long constricted newspapers, magazines, and television shows. We aren't going to run out of space in the blogosphere anytime soon. Feel free to make your post about how your toddler looks just like Suri Cruise as long as you'd like.

If you want to take your blog to the next level, though, it helps to have some sort of theme to the majority of your posts. People who work in public relations often advise their clients to become "experts" on a topic. When you write about a particular topic or theme regularly, you become a go-to person for others who are interested in the topic. They start to check in regularly, or whenever your subject is in the news, to see what you have to say. For examples of expert blogs, check out Engadget on technology, Apartment Therapy on decorating small spaces, Eater on New York City restaurants, and Vickie Howell's Purls of Wisdom about knitting over at the DIY network site, to name just a few.

If you'd like to write about a topic, you'll need to choose the right one for you. Here's some of the best advice we've heard:

Write about what you love. "Blog your passion," says Leslie Goldman, author of *Locker Room Diaries* and HuffPost blogger. "If you love dog grooming more than life itself, the blogs will write themselves and you'll never run out of topics."

Unfortunately, many of us aren't so sure what our passions are.

According to the Pew Internet and American Life Project 2006 survey of bloggers, we pretty much write about what we know.

37% = "my life and experiences"

22% = other

11% = politics and government

7% = entertainment

6% = sports

5% = general news and current events

5% = business

4% = technology

2% = religion or spirituality

1% = a specific hobby or illness

So here are some ways to figure it out. Watch yourself as you read a newspaper or magazine. What stories catch your eye? When do you turn up the volume on the radio and tell the carpool to shut up? You can even look back through photo albums from when you were a kid. What did you love to play with? What kinds of books did you hide under the covers at night? If you lose track of time when you're talking about a topic, that's a hint that maybe you'd like to write about it. The great thing about blogging is that it's not subject to the same practicalities we encounter when we try to make a living. Just because you went into pharmaceutical marketing rather than studying Fabergé eggs doesn't mean you can't blog about Peter Carl Fabergé to your heart's content.

Be specific enough to create a community—at least at first.
Wired editor in chief Chris Anderson's blog and 2006 book, *The Long Tail,* pointed out a new business phenomenon: The mass market is disappearing. In the past, any given music album had to be popular enough to justify shelf space in every retail store— from Bangor to LA—that sold music. So we wound up with a few albums that a lot of people liked all right. Thanks to the infinite space available on the web, though, the mass market is being replaced by millions of niche markets. Since the costs of storage in one central location and a web page noting the album's existence are so low, it now makes sense for online retailers to stock copies of any CD that a few people will like a lot. If you simply offer music for download, as opposed to a physical CD, the economics are even better. It's hard to compete with the big boys (Wal-Mart, for instance). But there's money to be made by offering niche products that people are passionate about.

Good blog topics take this phenomenon into account. "Moms" is too broad a category for most bloggers to gain traction with and build a community around. "Accountant moms who work from home" is more focused. "Sports" can be best tackled by ESPN and its ilk, but "Maryland high school lacrosse" will attract followers. You should have a good idea of who will read your blog. Who is she? Why does she care about the topic? What are you going to offer her to make a read worth her time? On the other hand . . .

Choose something broad enough to sustain your interest. By definition, a blog requires regular updating. You don't need to post many times a day (though you can, and many bloggers do), but if you want to build a readership, choose a topic you'll be able to post about at least once a week for the foreseeable future. Not sure if you're on the right track? Jot down your ideas for the first few posts you'd like to write. If you can come up with ten in a few minutes, you're good to go.

Of course, it's quite possible that your blog will evolve over time. Your kids will grow up. Your politics might change. You might discover go-kart racing. So it goes. With blogs, no editor will tell you that you can't change or add topics. If you write things worth reading and you're consistent about posting, over time your readership will evolve and expand with you. Indeed, some of the best-known blogs have broadened their focus over time. Huff-Post had a very political focus at first but now covers everything from entertainment to green living.

Then again, with a billion people out there on the web, you might find that the community of accountant moms who work from home and love go-kart racing is bigger than you ever thought.

What Makes a Good Blog Title?

Ah, the art of titles. Some of us have been involved in other book projects before this one. The pressure to come up with a good book title usually has our fingernails looking like they were attacked by blind wolverines by the time we smack something on the dust jacket and hope it works. You know how your mother said you shouldn't judge a book by its cover? Well, people do. A good title like *The Four-Hour Workweek* can make a book leap off the shelf. Lots of people simply use their own name as their blog title, but if you decide to give your blog a title, you want that title to do a lot of heavy lifting for you. Ideally, the title should:

Avoid the "huh?" factor. Be clear. You want your target reader to know instantly that this is the blog for her.

Be short. No one wants to list a three-line blog in their blogroll. The Huffington Post is better than "Arianna Huffington and Friends Muse on Politics, Life, and Everything Else."

Stand out. We don't have to tell you that the blogosphere is crowded. A regularly updated, thoughtful blog will naturally

---

GENIUS BLOG NAMES

Some of these blogs/websites are no longer active, but the names do make us want to visit them: Wonkette, Instapundit, Invisible Adjunct, Stuff White People Like, Ladies Who Launch, Purls of Wisdom, The Hippocratic Oaf, One Thousand Words (on photos), The Budget Fashionista, Escape from Obesity, Tales from the Stirrups (a fertility blog), Pink is the New Blog, Wokking Mum (on cooking), Daddy's Little Tax Credits gather readers over time. But a catchy title (tweaking a cliché, referencing a pun or well-known phrase) helps a lot.

Should I Write Under My Own Name?

> A lot of people ask me if they should blog under a
> pseudonym. They ask me because I started writing under
> a pseudonym eight years ago, and it ended up being such
> a mess that I turned it into my real name. So I advise
> everyone to start out using their real name.
> —*Penelope Trunk, blogger and* Boston Globe *career columnist*

Many bloggers built their reputation by using their own name as their blog title. Others write titled blogs but still make their own names public (see Gina Trapani of Lifehacker). In general, the blogosphere thrives on transparency. That makes using your own name a good idea.

On the other hand, some situations call for anonymity. If you're trying to blow the whistle on abuses in a government agency or company but you want to keep your job, you will probably need to stay anonymous. If you work for an otherwise decent company that frowns upon or forbids blogging and you want to keep your job, you will need to stay anonymous. Anonymity can also let you write from a different perspective. *Forbes* senior editor Daniel Lyons entertained readers for over a year by assuming the persona of Steve Jobs in order to lampoon the Apple CEO.

Here's another reason to stay anonymous that occurs to most people way too late: If you are a teenager or college student writing about the various debauched things you and your friends do for fun, you should realize that someday you are going to grow up. Unless you've got a trust fund, you'll need to get a job. Prospective employers will Google your real name. They will not be amused when your manifesto on the best body shots you've ever done appears on the screen ("Oh, the Latvian indie actor with the tattoo of Joni Mitchell on his perfectly smooth chest! I taste the tequila every time I hear 'The Circle Game' ").

Even if you choose a pseudonym, though, you should know that most people aren't good at maintaining anonymity for long. Eventually you will slip and reveal your identity somewhere. Or you'll post information that's so specific that only you (and your Luddite coworker who persists in printing out all her e-mails and hence can be crossed off the suspect list) would know it.

The story of an anonymous blogger being unmasked is so common it's now an Internet cliché. Jessica Cutler, a.k.a. "Washingtonienne," was fired from her Capitol Hill job in 2004 after Wonkette (another blog; see the great-name list) revealed her identity. Ellen Simonetti, a.k.a. the "Queen of Sky," a Delta flight attendant, was fired later that year after her employer started tracking her anonymous travel blog. In 2007, pediatrician Robert P. Lindeman was asked on the stand during a malpractice case whether he was the blogger "Flea" who had written about a suspiciously similar trial, ridiculing the plaintiff's arguments. After admitting that he was, he wound up paying a sizable settlement to the family that was suing him. Unmasking may not be the end of your career. *Fortune*'s Stanley Bing has persisted in writing columns (and now blogging on his own website and for HuffPost) under his nom de plume, twelve years after being outed as CBS public relations executive Gil Schwartz. But there's no guarantee.

So here's our advice: Use a pseudonym if you want, but keep in mind that blog posts are available to anyone with a computer and stay accessible long after you've posted them. Ask yourself what would happen if someone found out that you're the poster behind your blog. Embarrassment? A reprimand? Losing your job? Legal action? If it's a consequence that you're not prepared to handle, then maybe you should find a less public way to deal with the issues you want to blog about.

Blog Infrastructure

After you've got a topic and a title (or have decided to keep it simple and use your name), it's time to start creating your blog.

The first thing you'll need to do is choose your blogging service. We've listed some of the most popular ones here. This is by no means an exhaustive list. But it's a start. Each website has more information on setup.

Blogger (www.blogger.com, owned by Google). This is a good first choice for most people. It's free and easy. To start, you just fill in a bit of information and can begin blogging in minutes. Since your blog will be hosted on Blogger's server, you don't need to worry about purchasing a domain name, fixing bugs, or maintaining your own server. If you didn't understand that last sentence, then this is definitely the service for you.

Blogger was started by a San Francisco–based company called Pyra Labs in August 1999. The team that created it limped along through the dot-com crash until 2002, when Google scooped it up. So to use Blogger in its current incarnation, you will have to create a Gmail account if you don't already have one. This isn't a big problem for most people as Gmail is also free, and no one requires that you check it. Your blog address will be yourblog.blogspot.com.

Blogger has several basic templates, and options to create a customized one. The posting screen is fairly intuitive—with easy buttons to add links, images, and video—and you can turn on security features that ward off spammers.

There are a few downsides to using a popular hosted blog service. For starters, you'll have to live with the "blogspot" in your address (if you want your own domain name, use a service you host yourself—see below for information about WordPress.org and Movable Type). You're also at the mercy of someone else's server. If they choose to shut the service down, your blog could disappear. But Google pledges not to be evil and doesn't appear to be going anywhere anytime soon. Famous customers: Google (duh) and MC Hammer.

TypePad (www.typepad.com, owned by Six Apart). This service bills itself as the blogging software for professionals and small businesses. As with Blogger, your blog will be hosted on the TypePad server. Unlike Blogger, it will cost you, from $4.95 per month for a basic package to $89.95 per month for "business class." TypePad thinks there's an upside to charging. "You (not advertisers) are our customer," they note. "Since TypePad is a paid service, advertising spam will never appear on your blog." They also claim this fee model gives them a leg up in customer service. If you anticipate getting a lot of traffic but don't want to pony up for server space yourself, TypePad has the back-end capacity to handle blogs of any size. Famous customer: Martha Stewart (the Martha Blog).

LiveJournal (www.livejournal.com, owned by SUP). Like Blogger, this San Francisco–based company appeared on the scene in 1999, when founder Brad Fitzpatrick was looking for a way to keep his high school friends updated on his life. LiveJournal combines blogging with social networking and stresses that LJ blogs are part of a larger community (the company has an advisory board that bloggers can be elected to). Users designate "friends" and can be updated on friends' recent activities. Setup is free. LiveJournal has gone through several owners recently. Six Apart purchased it from Danga Interactive in January 2005, then spun it off to SUP, a Russian company, in December 2007. Famous customer: Billy Corgan of Smashing Pumpkins.

WordPress (www.wordpress.org; www.wordpress.com for the hosted version). Started in 2003, this is an open-source program. That means the source code is available, is free, and is constantly being reworked by a community of programmers. WordPress exists in two forms. In the best-known, dot-org version, you download the software and host the service on your own site. It is fully customizable, which is great if you're a programmer or have one on staff. The technology can be easily folded into your existing website with no loss of brand consistency. WordPress eventually realized, though, that this requirement that you have your own domain name and server was a fairly big barrier to entry for newbie bloggers. So the programmers who created the open-source software also started the dot-com version, which is hosted and free (like Blogger). Famous customer: Ford Motor Company.

Movable Type (www.movabletype.com, owned by Six Apart). This service is free to download for personal use; if you are a business using the blog to help drive revenue, commercial licenses start at $295.95 for five users ($99.95 for nonprofits). Like the dot-org version of WordPress, you will need your own domain name and server; Six Apart provides technical support. The company's sweet spot is larger multiuser blogs, which is one of the reasons we use it. Famous customer: HuffPost.

Other options: Social networking sites MySpace and Facebook have blogging capability already built into their member profile pages. If you have a full profile and lots of friends on these sites, then you'll have an instant audience for your blog.

For a more complete listing of available blog software programs, see the Wikipedia entry for "weblog software," which is updated more often than this book (en.wikipedia.org/wiki/Blog _software).

Pimp My Blog: More Ways to Tell Your Story

Like any other form of communication, blogging has inspired subgenres and spin-offs, and also incorporates some other communication concepts. Want to sound savvy? We define a few terms you'll hear from time to time:

Tumblelogs: These are short-form blogs that are heavy on multimedia (art, photos, sound clips). They're popular with artists and are enabled by software such as Tumblr (www.tumblr.com) which makes it easy to post one item at a time.

Podcasts: These are digital media sound clips meant to be played over the Internet or on portable media players (e.g., the iPod). Some bloggers incorporate podcasts into their posts. For instance, if you interview a leading psychologist for your parenting blog, you might write up your notes from the interview but also record the interview and include that as a podcast so readers can listen in. Reporters often dispatch podcasts from hurricane or war zones, where it's hard to get an uninterrupted half hour to type. Readers can download podcasts and listen to them on the go.

To create a podcast, you'll need a microphone (many new computers already have one) and some recording software. You can buy high-end professional sound editing software, but a good option for experimenting with podcasting for free is an open-source program called Audacity (audacity.sourceforge.net).

Vlogs: These are video logs. In addition to, or rather than, posting text, the blogger posts a video file. Some people create these files through their cell phones or other video cameras, or you can purchase an accessory camera for your computer (several companies—such as Lenovo and Microsoft—now make them for less than $50). There are a number of benefits to vlogging. Humans are visual creatures, and seeing the person who is blogging helps create a more intimate situation. Thanks to faster Internet connections, video files now load quickly. They can also be posted on YouTube to build buzz. Downside: When we're blogging in our pajamas, we'd often prefer there be no visual record.

Photolog or sketchblog: Like a blog, but with a focus on photos or other visual images for more intimacy and personal context.

Anatomy of a Blog Post

After you've chosen a topic and a blogging service, it's time to set up your blog and write your first post. Here's one of Arianna's, with the components labeled. We'll define them below.

❶ Template. This is the basic background for your blog. Services such as Blogger allow you to choose from a small number of templates that are easy on the eyes. But most people try to upgrade to something a bit more snazzy shortly after they get the blogging bug. There's a simple reason for this: There are only a few default templates for each blogging software program. There are millions of blogs. So if you choose a standard template, your blog will look just like a million others.

Some people consider this a downside. On the other hand, blogging software companies do tend to hire designers who know what they're doing. If you decide to upgrade, be sure to run your template by somebody who knows what they're doing unless you have an eye for these things. The world needs many things right now, but one of them is not a red blog with fuchsia text and flashing graphics of lightning bolts. To find a good designer, e-mail the hosts of blogs you like, or put an ad on Craigslist (or, if you've got lots of traffic, your own blog). Expect to pay for this service.

❷ Header. Your logo. This goes on top of every page at your site, so that if a reader wanders into a past post that's no longer on your home page, she'll know where she is. The basic blogging services have decent ones, or again, you can design your own.

❸ Titles. The headline on your post. Coming up with good article titles is tough. That's why it's a major part of the job description for some editors at newspapers and magazines. The upside is that you'll get better at it over time. Like the name of your blog, a post title should be short, clear, and catchy. If someone

①

② ARIANNA HUFFINGTON | BIO | I'M A FAN OF THIS BLOGGER

③ # What's That Sound? Why It's the Further Lowering of the Bar on Iraq

④ Posted November 25, 2007 | 11:01 PM (EST)

⑤ **Read More:** Donald Rumsfeld, George W. Bush, Iraq Spin, Iraq Surge, Iraq Surge Results, Long Hard Slog, Lowering Of Expectations For Iraq, New York Times, Ryan Crocker, Success Of The Surge, War In Iraq, Breaking Politics News

---

ARIANNA HUFFINGTON

I'M A FAN OF THIS BLOGGER (GET EMAIL ALERTS)

⑥ Arianna Huffington is the co-founder and editor-in-chief of The Huffington Post, a nationally syndicated columnist, and author of twelve books. She is also co-host of "Left, Right & Center," public radio's popular political roundtable program.

In May 2005, she launched The Huffington Post, a news and blog site that has quickly become one of the most widely-read, linked to, and frequently-cited media brands on the Internet.

In 2006, she was named to the Time 100, Time Magazine's list of the world's 100 most influential people.

NEWS SOURCES

ABC

Al Jazeera

AOL News

Associated Press (Huffington Post)

BBC

Bloomberg

Boston Globe

Huffington Post in the New York Times

NPR

Off The Bus (Huffington Post)

PBS NewsHour

Newsweek

People

Politico

Radar

Democracy Arsenal

Firedoglake

Gawker

Hotline On Call (National Journal)

Hullabaloo

Informed Comment

Instapundit

James Wolcott (Vanity Fair)

Wonkette

COLUMNISTS

Jonathan Alter

Eric Alterman

Sidney Blumenthal

Eric Boehlert

Ron Brownstein

Joe Conason

David Corn

asked you what your post was about and you had to tell them as you were racing out the door, what would you say? That's a good starting point for thinking about titles. Feel free to have fun with it. People can remember a good headline for years (for instance, the *New York Post* classic "Headless Body in Topless Bar.")

❹ **Date/Time.** If you're blogging on a hot topic, it's good to be first. This stamp tells the world when your brilliant insight went live. Some programs allow you to change the date and time, so if you're blogging at work, all of your posts can look like they were written at 5:30 P.M.

❺ **Tags.** These are labels that make it easier to find posts about a certain subject. When HuffPost bloggers file, they create a list of tags or keywords—the words you use to search for a given subject—that describe the topics covered in that post. If you're writing a post about reactions to a round of layoffs at a corporation in your town, potential tags might include *layoffs, economy, jobs, recession, unemployment,* the name of the company, the names of local politicians quoted in the piece, the industry in question, etc. As long as the tag is genuinely related to your piece, throw it in. When readers come to a blog home page, they often search for a particular topic. If that topic is one of your tags, then your post will come up.

Of course, this doesn't mean the reader will necessarily click on your post. Lots of bloggers choose popular tags (e.g., *Barack Obama, Iraq, Angelina Jolie*). While readers are more likely to search for popular tags, they are less likely to read your post over the one thousand others that show up on the screen. Rare tags (e.g., *Fabergé eggs*) are searched for by fewer people, but the few fans that do search for them will probably read what you have to say.

❻ Bio. This is the "about me" section of the blog. It's what you want the world to know about you. It's not a formal résumé, though it's a good idea to establish that you know what you're talking about. Do you write about parenting? Mention your kids (or say why you're writing about parenting if you *don't* have children). Blogging about divorce? Mention your own, or your parents', or whatever inspired you to choose this topic. Readers love a story. Why are you the right person to keep this blog? They also want to know a few details about you. Where do you live? What kind of industry do you work in? When are you happiest? Here's another tip: Choose a good photo. If you ever turn up missing or are accused of some heinous crime, this is the one that will be all over the news.

❼ Blogroll. In the old days before cyberspace, people would show who their friends were by exchanging autograph books to sign. A blogroll is a digital version of that. It is featured on your blog home page and consists of links to your favorite blogs. A blogroll shows readers what interests you and (most likely) where you're getting a lot of your information.

Other components not pictured here include:

Sidebar. Other information besides your post on the page. Can be links to other top posts.

Photos and art. Most newspaper and magazine articles include a photo, chart, or other visual element to draw the reader in and break up large blocks of text. This is a good idea for blogs, too. You can upload a photo from your files to illustrate a piece. Blogging programs such as TypePad and Blogger make it easy to insert files. Keep in mind, though, that many professional photos are copyrighted. If you plan to use a lot of visual images, consider joining a photo service such as iStockphoto, which allows you to download lots of images for a small fee. See the section on fair use and copyright below.

Pull quotes. These are quotes—things people said, passages from another blog or article—that you are highlighting. Like photos, pull quotes provide an element of visual interest for the reader. Separating a quote from the rest of the text allows the reader to consider a quote on its own and then consider your analysis.

Linking. You want people to visit your blog, right? Other people want readers to come to their blogs as well. Providing links is the blogosphere equivalent of doing unto others as you would have them do unto you.

Here's the etiquette. If you reference an idea or bit of information from another website, you should try to provide a link to it. Not only is this giving credit to those whose work you're citing, it allows the reader to instantly check your facts and judge for himself if that source is worth listening to. Having links in your posts gives you credibility. It shows that you're not making stuff up.

Until recently, bloggers had to type some rather complicated instructions to insert links in their posts (it involved strings of characters like "</a>"). These days, most blog software programs take a hint from user-friendly word processing programs and don't require you to know any language besides English. Blogger, for instance, has a little link button on top of the space where you enter posts (near the italicize "*i*" button and the "**b**" bold button; it looks like a chain link). If you highlight a word or phrase and then hit the "link" button, the program will prompt you to enter the website address. When you preview or publish your post, this should show up as different-colored text, indicating that if you click on that word, you'll be directed to another website.

There's no hard and fast rule about how many links a good post should have. Maybe your idea sprang from your noggin fully formed, like Athena from Zeus's head. But if not, chances are you'll be referencing at least one current event, product, or friend who was involved in the particular issue you're writing about. There's no reason to create a whole fence of links. Some people in the throes of search engine optimization (which we'll talk about later in chapter 3, "Getting Noticed") will link to things like the Wikipedia entry for "baseball" when they're writing about going to last night's game. But in general, links are both a way of giving credit and a way of making life easier for your reader. If it took you a while to find something, be considerate and save your readers the trouble.

By the way, here's a tip you'll hear from multiple bloggers. Your traffic can rise a hundredfold in a day if a popular blogger (Perez Hilton, Instapundit) links to you. One way to encourage that? Link to some of their posts. You never know. The web is a freewheeling place. It just might work.

The best links, usually, are to things the reader would never have found otherwise. Fred Pruitt's Rantburg blog specializes in interesting information from obscure military and regional sources. Meanwhile Caterina Fake's blog—probably my favorite of the largely nonpolitical, day-in-the-life blogs—has posts on things like what to do in Finland, full of links and reader comments. In both cases, the selection of links has to do with the "personal voice" thing: Fred and Caterina are very different people. Both have built blogs around their own knowledge and interests, instead of trying to imitate someone else, and the result, in both cases, has been something very interesting and useful indeed.

—GLENN REYNOLDS, A.K.A. INSTAPUNDIT

Comments. Hearing what other people have to say about your ideas and stories is half the fun of blogging. You should definitely allow comments on your blog. We'll write more about encouraging comments and building a community in chapter 5.

Fair Use and Copyright

Since blogging is such a new addition to the communication landscape, it should be no surprise that the legal issues are still under construction. "The big picture is that blogging advances an open and robust discussion of issues that are of interest to our society," says Mary Mulligan, a partner at Friedman Kaplan Seiler and Adelman LLP who often advises Internet service providers and has practiced in the copyright area. "Bloggers are generally protected by the First Amendment because they're advancing our communication and advancing public discussion." Whether in person or online, you have the right to free speech.

However, you can run afoul of certain areas (Mulligan stresses that this is not legal advice; if you want specific advice on your blog, you should consult your own lawyer).

- **Don't blog on your employer's nickel or using the office network.** Not only are you supposed to be doing your actual job, employees have few privacy rights when they are on the clock or using their employers' equipment. Many folks are employed "at will" these days, meaning that you or the employer can terminate your employment at any time and for any reason. So even if you are keeping a blog outside of office hours, you could in theory be dismissed if your employer feels that your blog reflects negatively on the company. Mulligan notes that this is why some people blog anonymously, but, as discussed earlier in this chapter, there's no guarantee you'll stay anonymous for long. When in doubt, ask for your employer's policy on blogging. If it's OK, try to stay within any guidelines specified (for instance, not mentioning your company, or putting a disclaimer on your website that the opinions are yours and not your employer's).
- **Don't use your blog to purposefully target and defame someone.** For instance, if you start a blog whose sole function is to spread vile rumors about your ex, your ex might be able to sue you. There are broader exceptions for targeting public figures (if the plaintiff is a public figure, he or she has to prove actual malice). But in general, it pays to be truthful in real life and on the web.
- **Be familiar with copyright law and the idea of what constitutes "fair use."** Many articles, photos, and the like are copyrighted by either their author or the publication that ran the content. When something is copyrighted, it

For a deeper discussion of blogging legal issues, check out the website of the Electronic Frontier Foundation (www.eff.org). EFF is a civil liberties group that defends bloggers' rights in the digital world. The website gives an overview of issues including intellectual property, defamation, privacy issues, election law, labor law, adult material, and more.

means that other people can't use it for their own purposes without permission. But there are exceptions for "fair use." This is the principle that allows a book reviewer to quote from a book she's reviewing without getting the author's permission. "If you find something interesting that you would like to comment on, typically short quotations would be protected by fair use," Mulligan says. Unfortunately, or fortunately, depending on your perspective, "There are no strict rules for fair use." The standard is still evolving for the Internet age.

Here's what you need to know. In general, courts apply a four-part test. A court would consider the purpose and character of the use. Is it for education and discussion? Or are you reprinting content you didn't pay for just to draw people to your site so you can make money through ads? A court would consider the nature of the copyrighted work and then the amount or portion used. In general, copying the entire work or copying its core would probably not be found to be fair use. There's no strict word count here because while few people would blink at quoting a hundred words from a book, quoting the entirety of a one-hundred-word poem is a different matter. The final factor is the effect on the market or potential market for the work. If someone makes her living selling a brochure about how to build a better mousetrap and you put most of the brochure online without permission, this would probably not be fair use, as you are destroying the market for this person's work.

To stay on the safe side, only reprint as much content as you need, be sure to credit the source, and use copyrighted material for discussion purposes only. If you do want to use a longer portion of someone's work, you should write the author or the publication for permission. Sometimes people do want to see their ideas broadly distributed and will be willing to give permission for free or for a small fee.

In general, though, most bloggers don't need to be too worried about the legality of what they're doing. The Founding Fathers wrote the First Amendment in order to protect our ability to float new ideas and hold our leaders accountable. Blogs bring new voices into the discussion and provide even more checks on the system—which most people think is a good thing. As long as you're expressing your own opinions and trying to advance the discussion as truthfully as possible, you'll be fine.

HOW BLOGGING CHANGED THE GAME: IMMEDIACY + REACTIVITY = POLITICS NOT AS USUAL

BOB CREAMER, POLITICAL CONSULTANT AND HUFFPOST BLOGGER

Frankly, I began doing a regular blog on HuffPost because I thought it would help promote my book, *Listen to Your Mother—Stand Up Straight: How Progressives Can Win*. It did. But it rapidly became clear to me that the blog could have as much effect on the political dialogue in and of itself.

As a longtime political organizer I understood objectively how powerful the medium of the blogosphere had become, but I didn't get it subjectively until I started to write one.

For what it's worth, here are some of the things I've learned in the process.

Start a conversation. The unique thing about the blogging medium is that it triggers immediate response—it starts an online conversation. And I think I've been most successful when I think of my column on HuffPost as a conversation starter—the way you'd raise an issue at a party, in a class, or at the water cooler. The best blogs are written with the intention of engaging active participants in conversation, not just passive consumers of information. My wife [Illinois congresswoman Jan Schakowsky] used to say that one of the reasons she ran for Congress was so instead of yelling at the TV, she could yell on the TV. Blogs give everyone the ability to participate in and shape the dialogue.

Learn how people hear what you say. As a political consultant I admit to having an addiction to focus groups. I like seeing how people actually hear what we say as political communicators. Blogs provide the same instantaneous feedback. Sometimes you think you are starting one conversation and find that what people actually heard you say leads to an entirely different conversation. And, as is the case with all communication, many times people listen to the words you write but really hear the music of context or emotion that surrounds them—either in the piece itself or in the environment where your words land.

My most well-read blogs are almost always about something people are already thinking about—usually breaking news. They are aimed at throwing some gasoline on an already smoldering fire of reader interest and sparking a response.

Each column on the blog is aimed at making one key point. It's intended to state the point and then prove the point, not to sashay through a set of ruminations on a general subject.

The headline is intended to state the point I'm trying to make in a straight-ahead but intriguing statement. Its goal is to succinctly make the argument at the same time it creates interest in learning more. I think my best-read column on HuffPost was titled *Top Ten Reasons Why Obama Defeated Clinton for the Democratic Nomination.* This piece was written long before the outcome of the battle for the Democratic nomination was officially settled. It argued that Obama had in fact beaten Clinton and was intended to interest the reader in finding out why.

The lede paragraph restates and expands on the basic argument implicit in the headline. I generally try to use the standard journalistic form. Sometimes the lede actually lasts several paragraphs, but my goal is to ensure that by the time the reader has read the headline and lede, he or she is clear about my basic argument.

The body is intended to prove the headline and lede. It might use a simple narrative argument, but I usually find it useful to break up the body using numbered points, bullets, or bold type. In general I think arguments are easier to consume if they are broken down into nuggets of fact or narrative. I am also a big fan of short paragraphs that break up copy and limit the amount of "gray" on the page. They are much less intimidating and draw the reader along.

The conclusion restates the basic message of the piece and almost always includes some call to action. For me blogs are about asking people to respond—either in a comment or in action they take in real life.

I find that I get more response when the blog involves symbolic communication— stories or palpable examples—or compelling data, not simply rhetoric. Of course, that's one of the basic rules of all political communication, but it's especially important if you're writing to get a response, not just to make a point. The goal of political communication (and I write *political* blogs) is to engage the emotions, not just the mind—to change the way people feel, not just what they think.

Try to make the blog memorable. I find there are at least four rules that are useful in making something memorable:

1. **To be "sticky," a message has to relate directly to the reader's personal experience.** It has to make the reader nod in acknowledgment or laugh in recognition. It

needs to connect with the reader's everyday experience. Abstract political rhetoric is *not* memorable.

Memorable messages don't just make you *think* about a subject—they make you feel, taste, smell, or hear the content. They make you *experience* the content. A memorable message about pollution doesn't tell you about the concept of a polluted waterway—it describes a polluted waterway: its smell, its color, its toxicity.

2. **A message is more memorable if it makes the reader react emotionally.** We are much more likely to remember something we feel than something we simply think. It may make someone laugh, it may make them mad, it may make them cry—but one way or another it makes them react emotionally.

3. **Memorable messages often include an element of surprise.** They include the unexpected.

4. **Confusion leads to distraction.** If we don't understand a subject or the relevance of what is being described in a message, we begin to tune it out. It goes in one ear and out the other.

CHAPTER 3

GETTING NOTICED

> You have to sell your blog. It doesn't matter how
> substantive your piece is if you can't catch the reader's
> eye—and then hold their attention for a few minutes.
> —*Brandon Friedman, author of* The War I Always Wanted
> *and HuffPost blogger*

So you've created a blog. Now what? We're guessing you want the world to know about it. This chapter is about building that elusive concept known as buzz.

Bloggers who are serious about getting noticed ask two questions:

- Who is visiting my blog?
- How can I attract more visitors?

While the latter is more art than science, we'll cover some good ways to figure out both. Getting noticed is one of the most rewarding aspects of blogging, even if it's not necessarily rewarding in the monetary sense. Few people get rich off blogging, though some earn enough to pay for their high-speed Internet access or, failing that, a beer to drown their sorrows in. The last part of this

Buzz generally refers to word-of-mouth marketing—that is, what people are talking about as they hum like little worker bees through their daily lives. In a world saturated with ads, people like to rely on recommendations from other humans. When someone e-mails or calls and says, "You have got to see this," that's buzz.

chapter will talk about how to use your blog to generate income or, possibly, a new line of work.

Who Is Visiting My Blog?

If you just started blogging, the answer to this question is most likely "nobody." Maybe your mom checks in from time to time. Your spouse might give it a look if she's feeling bad about that whole shoebox-of-valuable-baseball-cards-into-the-recycling-bin incident. But that's okay. You didn't learn to swim with network news cameras trained on you, and you probably shouldn't learn to blog with an Olympic-sized audience either. The latter part of this chapter will tell you how to bump up your numbers. In the meantime, you'll want to know what the numbers are, so you can deal with them for what they are.

Before we talk about how to measure traffic, we need to define a few words you may hear batted around: *hits, page views, visits,* and *visitors* (both unique and repeat).

A hit is a web browser's request for information from a server. A browser requests every file on a blog separately. In plain English, this means that any time a visitor looks at your web page, they're going to register multiple hits—one for every file on the page. If you have five pictures, this is five hits (plus hits for the basic site). Consequently, hits are a pretty useless measure of blog traffic, though you can generate some impressive numbers to brag about to your less tech-savvy friends.

Page views and visits are more helpful for figuring out the actual size and nature of your audience. A page view is exactly what it sounds like—**every time a visitor opens a page in your blog,** and presumably focuses her eyeballs on it, **this is a view.**

The first visit to your home page is one view. If the reader clicks on a past post, thus opening a new page, this is a second view. If the reader then returns to your home page, this is a third view.

If you've got a "sticky" blog—that is, one that people linger in for a while—your page view number will be much higher than your number of visits. **A visit is when someone comes to your site.** If she opens multiple pages, she will generate a high number of page views, but that's still one visit. If she goes away for a while but comes back to your blog later in the day, this can be a second visit. But she's still the same visitor. When a site measures **unique visitors,** this is approximately **the number of different people who visit your site in a given period of time** (often a month). We say approximately because if you and your spouse share a computer and you both visit the same sites during your separate surfing sessions, this will register as only one visitor if you use the same browser. But given the plethora of personal computers out there, unique visitors is a pretty good indicator of how many people read your blog. Repeat visitors are people (technically, their browsers) who come back to your site during a given period of time. While you want a high number of unique visitors, repeat visitors is an important measure, too. A high number of repeat visitors means that when people visit your blog, they like it enough to come back.

Here's one way to think about this. You, a visitor, may pay a visit to an art museum on a Monday. Each gallery you wander into is a page view. Each painting you look at while you're in the gallery is a hit. So that one visit might generate ten page views and a hundred hits. If you come back to the museum on Tuesday, that's a second visit—but you are still the same visitor. You've simply become a repeat one.

Traffic's Not a Dirty Word: How to Measure What You're Getting

A few tools can help you figure out how many unique visitors are visiting you. These three popular ones are all "hosted," meaning that the companies maintain the software on their own servers. If you're running a blog on your own server (rather than through a hosted service like Blogger), there are a few other programs, such as Webalizer, that you can use. But these three do the trick for most people.

Site Meter (sitemeter.com). This tool comes in two versions: the basic free one, and a premium one that starts at $6.95 per month. You create an account, and then Site Meter gives you a unique code for your site. You incorporate this code into the HTML for each page you want tracked. This sounds complicated, though Site Meter promises detailed instructions for this step for every major commercial blogging and web hosting program. After you do this, Site Meter will generate statistics for you including total number of visits and page views, the average length of a visit, the average number of visits per day, and how many people have visited in the last hour, day, and week. In the free version, a little Site Meter counter will be visible on your blog (you can choose from several graphics). The paid version has an invisible option.

StatCounter (statcounter.com). StatCounter is also free in its basic version, though the company requests that you upgrade to a paid version if you start to get more than nine thousand page loads per day. The paid versions start at $9 per month. Like Site Meter, you have to include code in your HTML (and, like Site Meter, StatCounter provides instructions). The generated web statistics are a little more interesting, though, with such intriguing features as a Google map of recent visitor activity. StatCounter also offers the option—even in the free version—to keep your counter invisible. If you want a counter on your site, the graphics can be customized.

Google Analytics (google.com/analytics). Since Google is involved in everything else on the web, it's no surprise that the company offers visitor tracking and analysis as well. Google Analytics is free for the first five million page views (and if you've got that, more power to you). It's free for unlimited page views if you also have a Google AdWords account. (There's more information on Google AdWords later in this chapter.) To use the software, you'll need a Google account (i.e., your Gmail account, also free). Statistics displays are user-friendly and thorough, though Google Analytics is particularly optimized for sites that are trying to have visitors buy things or, not coincidentally, click on Google AdWords.

How Else Can I Figure Out If People Are Talking About Me?

Figuring out how many visits you're scoring is one thing—you also want to know how influential you are. You could spend all day reading blogs to see if other people are mentioning your posts, but this wouldn't leave any time for posting.

A more efficient way is to create a Google web alert (google.com/alerts) for your name, or the name you blog under, and your blog name. Any time either is mentioned on your or other websites, Google will e-mail you a link. One bit of advice: It's fine to celebrate every mention and visit every site that mentions you, but be a little cool about the fact that you've got a web alert set up. It can be a little creepy when a source we've written about multiple times is always the first one to post a comment on any thread that mentions him or her.

If you're not a total narcissist, you might also create Google Alerts for topics that interest you as a way of seeing what other people are writing, and maybe being inspired yourself.

How Can I Attract More Visitors? Learn the "Buzz Basics"

> The best way to build a readership is to start blogging, and blog often and well on topics that interest you. Once you're under way, it's perfectly fine to e-mail better-known bloggers with links to posts that you think they may find particularly interesting. But "sell the post, not the blog" is good advice—you're much more likely to get linked with a post on a hot topic than with an e-mail that just says, "I've got a blog."
> —*Glenn Reynolds, a.k.a. Instapundit*

The best way to attract visitors is to create compelling content. There really is no substitute for this. But over the years, we've noticed three characteristics of posts that are the most likely to garner buzz. There are also a few basic web tools to help you attract new visitors to your site when you do write particularly buzz-worthy posts—but more on this a bit later in the chapter .

Write on top of the news. Whenever big news breaks, people will be searching for posts on the topic. If you've got ideas, or if you have special expertise in a hot news area, write quickly and get it out there.

All the News That's Fit to Blog: HuffPost Bloggers Making News

"I was at my desk when my partner called to tell me that Jerry Falwell had died [in May 2007]. As a prominent gay rights activist, he was like the Joker to my Batman. I had even debated him about the sexual orientation of Tinky Winky. This was a man who had claimed that gay and lesbian people were in some way responsible for 9/11. I hung up and didn't think at all. I just wrote. It felt urgent that I weigh in. I knew that being critical of him would be the obvious route and would not move anyone to think differently. Those who hated him still would and those who revered him would dismiss me.

"So instead I wrote about what I had learned from him—everything from how to be a more effective TV debater to how much influence the media has in creating demagogues like Falwell. It was not the approach people would have expected.

"It was done in fifteen minutes and posted a few minutes after that. It was one of the first pieces of commentary on the Internet. It was very, very timely. Hundreds of readers weighed in. On both sides of the issues.

"It was one of my best posts. I didn't overthink it. I moved quickly. And I offered a point of view that gave permission to those who disagreed to keep reading."

—JOAN GARRY, FORMER EXECUTIVE DIRECTOR OF GLAAD AND HUFFPOST BLOGGER

"I spent a lot of time writing about the cultural implications leading up to the *Sex and the City* film release. My pieces generated a lot of interest and my page views went up a lot. But the best feeling I got was when I started seeing my work being quoted on other sites and blogs as 'expert' information. I knew that I had taken my work to a whole new level when I was cited on an *Entertainment Weekly* blog and my site made the *Newsweek* site and magazine."

—MELISSA SILVERSTEIN, MEDIA CONSULTANT, AUTHOR OF WOMEN AND HOLLYWOOD BLOG AND HUFFPOST BLOGGER

Offer facts, not just opinion. Everyone loves citing statistics, facts, or quotes to back up their opinions. If you want to be noticed, try generating those. Interview your friend in Iowa who just lived through a tornado. Calculate how much oil Americans could save by telecommuting. Call up food banks in your area and see how many people showed up on a given Saturday. Then call back every Saturday for two months and ask the same question to see if there's a trend. This is basic, easy reporting—but it's like gold in the opinion-saturated blogosphere.

Give something a new spin. Certain opinions have been repeated so often that they become part of the cultural wallpaper. Writing about a class war between the "two Americas" (rich and poor) won't get much attention, but when Matt Miller proposed an intriguing thesis in *Fortune* in 2006 that there was a class war going on between the "lower uppers" (that is, the merely rich) and the "ultrarich," his piece was forwarded for weeks. If you can get a reader to think, "Wow, I haven't thought of it that way before," there's a good chance she'll forward your post, link to you, or post a comment.

Getting Noticed: The Tools

Compelling content comes first, but if you are creating compelling content, a few other activities will increase the chance that other humans will actually see it.

ALERT YOUR OWN NETWORKS

At least at the beginning, the majority of your blog readers will be people who know you personally. So whenever you post, you should reach out to these people to let them know there's new

I have a checklist I use to keep my posts interesting:

Am I being funny?

Am I giving smart information?

Am I revealing my character?

Am I telling stories?

Am I giving a picture of what it's like to live in New York City?

Am I linking to other bloggers?

—GRETCHEN RUBIN, AUTHOR OF THE HAPPINESS PROJECT BLOG AND HUFFPOST BLOGGER content. You can do this directly ("Hey, Mom, check out my blog!") or you can encourage your contacts to subscribe to an RSS feed of your blog. RSS stands for "Really Simple Syndication." The major blogging services allow you to create such feeds, which will send out new content to anyone who asks for it. This means that your friends and family won't have to remember to check back at your site—updates will come to their in-boxes automatically. If you and your friends use Twitter (www.twitter.com, a microblogging subscription service that delivers text-based messages via instant messaging and e-mail), you can send a short alert telling everyone that you've written a new post.

Here's some of the advice we give our bloggers when they submit a new piece for The Huffington Post. We find that these self-help publicity tips are a good way to start the ball rolling.

To: HuffPost Blogger
From: HuffPost Editors
Re: Getting Noticed

1. **E-Mail Lists:** Send a short note with a link to your post to any lists you're on—whether social organizations, extracurricular groups, or even just your typical family/friends list. Encourage them to comment. Create a community around your post and help it grow by starting with your own personal community. Encourage your friends to share it as well.

2. **Facebook/MySpace:** Share your post via Facebook or MySpace. Facebook makes it especially easy to share links through what they call "Posted Items." Your profile will then say that you've "shared a blog post" and will update your friends.

3. **Respond to Comments:** Just as readers love to see preexisting comments, they especially love to feel that the author of the post is engaged with the HuffPost community. Responding to comments on your own post helps the community grow around your post.

OPTIMIZE FOR SEARCH ENGINES

Say you're looking for a good chocolate chip cookie recipe. How would you find one? If you're like us, you'd go to Google (or possibly Yahoo! or MSN's search pages) and search for "chocolate chip cookie recipe." Links to several web pages of recipes would appear, and you'd click through to one of them—probably one near the top.

Unless people arrive at your blog via links (more on that in a moment), through a personal invitation, or because they're long-time fans of your site, they'll probably find you through a search engine. So you want your blog to come up near the top when a person searches for a topic you write about a lot.

The major search engines are constantly crawling the web, looking for new content. You'll show up on their radar screen soon enough if people link to you or if you keep updating. If you feel you're not showing up fast enough, you can submit the URL for your blog to **the major engines: Google** (www.google.com/addurl/), **Yahoo!** (https://siteexplorer.search.yahoo.com/submit) and **MSN** (search.msn.com/docs/submit.aspx). You can submit your blog to all the other search engines out there too, but most people have never heard of Shoula or Jayde and hey, life is short. Some companies promise to do this submission for you, but given that the major search engines employ many people to make sure the searches are thorough, we'd call this a waste of cash.

While showing up on a search engine's radar screen is pretty automatic, coming up near the top is not. Whole books have been written about search engine optimization (SEO), and people make their living helping websites retool to land that coveted first spot on Google for a given keyword (that is, the word or phrase someone is searching for).

There are **two basic approaches to boosting your ranking in a search.** The first is organic. Over time, if you **produce lots of good, relevant content** on a particular topic, people will link to you. If people link to you, and you have a lot of regularly updated content, then your search engine ranking will go up. No need to do anything else.

The other approach is a bit more aggressive. Many search engines take note of the **number of times you use a keyword as a measure of how relevant that keyword is to your particular page.** So if your blog posts use a keyword a lot (in the title, of course, but also in many of your sentences) this could, in theory, boost your ranking. On the other hand, simply repeating a keyword many times makes your post illegible to actual humans. If your purpose is to attract readers, that amounts to shooting yourself in the foot. **Moderation is key.**

Search engines definitely note how many times other people link to your site. If lots of people link to your site, then the search software perceives you as a good source of information. You could just hope this happens, or you can reach out to other bloggers to increase the chances that there will be multiple links to you floating around the blogosphere. There are several ways to do this.

First, you should **create a blogroll**—a list of links to other blogs you like on your home page. Tell these bloggers that you've done this, and ask them to link to you.

If you've been blogging for a while, you can **ask other bloggers to guest blog for you.** When another blogger posts on your site, they will definitely link to it from their own site and thus share their audience with you. If you've got a reputation as a strong writer, other bloggers might ask you to guest blog for them.

If you're trying to build up an audience, this is a good idea. You'll be able to link to your own site from the other site where you're blogging.

Become a good blogging neighbor. Send other bloggers content from your blog that they might find interesting. And, of course, link to and **comment on interesting fodder from other blogs.** In the blog world, there's a lot of mutual back-scratching when it comes to links. But even if other people don't link back to you, including useful links on your site seems to help boost your search engine ranking to some degree. You don't need to link to everything, but certainly link to anything you're citing from someone else, or information that might be difficult for readers to find on their own.

USE SHARING TOOLS SUCH AS YAHOO! BUZZ AND DIGG

The vast majority of blog posts will receive almost no attention whatsoever. But when a post starts getting buzz, certain new sharing services mean that it can suddenly catch fire. If you want

---

You Better Work It: Networking Your Blog

Put the URL in a tag on your e-mails. I made up postcards. Across the whole glossy front it says "Nice People CAN Finish First," with the blog URL underneath. On the back I have info about the blog and me. I hand them out wherever I go and leave them in appropriate places. Be consistent. Even if it feels like no one is reading your blog, post regularly. Interact with other bloggers. Leave comments on their posts. Invite them to guest post and see if you can be a guest on someone else's blog. I have a guest blogger or an interview with someone inspiring [once it was Perez Hilton] almost every week.

—DAYLLE DEANNA SCHWARTZ, LESSONS FROM A RECOVERING DOORMAT BLOG

to be noticed, this is a good thing. Here are a few of our favorites:

Yahoo! Buzz (buzz.yahoo.com): Run by Yahoo!, this program allows readers to find interesting posts and then tell Yahoo! and their friends about them. People can vote on the most buzzworthy story at the Yahoo! Buzz home page.

Digg (digg.com): Like Yahoo!, Digg asks users to find great content from around the web. When it's posted on Digg, other users have the opportunity to "digg" it. As with Yahoo!, since millions of people view the Digg home page, the most digged articles can quickly soar in views.

Delicious (delicious.com): Billing itself as a "social bookmarking site," Delicious lets you save bookmarks and share them with friends. You can look through other saved bookmark files and find fascinating sites that other people have recommended in different topic areas—much like the fun of hunting through a well-stocked bookstore.

We list a few more sharing tools in the resource section. The easiest way to take advantage of these sharing tools is to simply install the icons for them on your blog. That makes it easy for readers to click on the icon and thus submit your content to the sharing sites. When you tell your friends and family members about your new posts in your personal e-mails, you could hint that if they really loved you, they'd click on these icons. (It never hurts to ask.)

THINK LIKE A PUBLICIST

Like any other news outlet, we get a lot of press releases, publicity calls, and the like. We also have our own media relations expert, Mario Ruiz, whose advice on e-mail pitching is included in this chapter. What all this exposure to public relations tells us is that

ATTENTION YOU MIGHT NOT WANT

I got fired from *The New Republic.* The pretext for them firing me—it was actually about the war, even though the guy who fired me will go to his grave denying that simple truth—was the fact that I had launched a Blogspot blog called Too Hot for TNR when I was hungover after a party. It was up for three days, and read by absolutely no one besides ten friends of mine, before I got the can. Blogging can be dangerous.

—SPENCER ACKERMAN, SENIOR REPORTER, THE WASHINGTON INDEPENDENT AND HUFFPOST BLOGGER building buzz is a complicated game. Basically, you want your blog name mentioned—and recommended—in the most prominent places possible. Ideally, Oprah Winfrey will tell her audience that they have to visit your blog right now (and if she does, can you recommend this book on your blog? Please?). A feature on *Good Morning America* or *The Today Show* is considered a coup, as is the five-minute interview segment on *The Daily Show with Jon Stewart*. You'll notice that these are all television shows, and that's not a coincidence. For whatever reason, television has the power to compel us, zombie-like, to do things such as (you hope) visit your blog.

But radio and print aren't bad, either. A cover story in *The New York Times Magazine* would be marvelous publicity for your blog. A six-inch story in the *South Bend Tribune* is less fantastic, but even that is better than nothing, particularly if the story is positive. A prominent mention at a big blog such as HuffPost is great too. A popular radio host like (dare we say it?) Rush Limbaugh has a lot of clout with his audience. That's why they're called dittoheads. They do what he says.

To interest the media beast in your story, you need to think like a publicist. Publicists get to know the gatekeepers at major media outlets and then find ways to be useful. Getting to know the gatekeepers is—like everything else—a matter of networking. Write reporters who cover areas you blog about and send them your best content. Go to conferences or other events in your specialty area and meet the media types who show up. Post thoughtful comments on media websites.

Then, when big news happens in your specialty area, or when your blog is going to make news, offer yourself as an expert. Posting a video of yourself waxing eloquent will help television and

THE ART OF E-PITCHING

MARIO RUIZ, VICE PRESIDENT, MEDIA RELATIONS, THE HUFFINGTON POST

- **Make sure your subject headline is short and snappy,** and that the text of your e-mail quickly cuts to the chase.
  - ✔ Drop the lengthy intros and sign-offs, and bottom-line what it is you're trying to convey—whether it's an interesting point of view or a newsy nugget.
  - ✔ Stick to one or two lines, if possible. If they're interested, they'll click through to your blog.
  - ✔ Don't be afraid to be bold and to have an opinion (just make sure it's not long-winded).
- **Move fast.** Quickly respond to news of the day and rapidly turn around responses to stories your pitch is related to.
- **Be persistent.** Don't expect to hear back—if a blogger is interested he or she will most likely link without telling you. But don't e-mail a second time, unless you're offering an important exclusive and you need an answer.
- **Target your audience.**
  - ✔ Do your research. Know who writes about what. Technorati is great for information about who's covering what subjects.
  - ✔ There's a time for one-on-one pitching and there's a time for BCCing a larger group. If your item has news value, BCC is fine. If you're trying to convey your opinion, a one-on-one approach is more effective (in which case it's good to acknowledge your target's writings on the subject).
- **Build relationships.**
  - ✔ If a blog picks you up, e-mail a note to say thanks. Even if there's no response, everyone likes to be acknowledged.
  - ✔ If you're especially moved by something someone's written, e-mail them. Next time you hit them up for linking, they'll be more receptive.

- **E-mail addresses can be found.** Even if they're hidden, most often media targets and bloggers have their e-mail addresses posted somewhere online. Google is your best friend. Trial and error helps too.
- **Don't forget mainstream media.** PR is more than just getting linked to; it's also about getting referred to in newspapers, magazines, TV, and radio.
- **There's no such thing as perfect PR.** A snarky pickup is fine; it's better to get noticed than to be ignored. Grow thicker skin.
- **Be polite.** If someone posts your work without crediting or linking, e-mail them, but be friendly. That adage about honey vs. vinegar is true.

radio producers know you can actually speak well enough for broadcast and don't have two heads. You can also have some snazzy quotes ready to go—e-mail them to a reporter who you think might mention your blog. While you're at it, give the reporter some facts he might not be aware of. And include the name of your blog. Even if it doesn't work the first time, you'll be on the reporter's or producer's radar screen. She may call you up next time if you've got a unique angle—like being a yoga instructor who works with returning combat troops, or a real estate agent who helps people through the foreclosure process. Daily reporters in particular are always looking for stories. Try brainstorming a few stories that would involve quoting you as an expert, and e-mail these pitches to the reporters you know.

You can also submit op-eds on your blog's area of expertise to newspapers, magazines, or other blogs. If your blog is really starting to get some buzz, you could hire a part-time publicist to increase overall exposure.

All in all, marketing a blog bears a lot of resemblance to marketing a book or album. If you know an author or musician, take her out for coffee and grill her on publicity ideas. It's hard work trying to stand out in our five-hundred-channel, 112 million–blog universe. But people still do it. Watch TV and read the papers critically for a few weeks to see what publicity ideas have been working. Then go ahead and give it a shot.

Making Money with Your Blog

No blogging guide is complete without a section on making money from your new gig. When people think of a blogging business model, the first thing that comes to mind is that they'll run ads on their site. But, in fact, the economics of this route are rather dicey—so don't quit your day job expecting that cash will fly into your pockets the second you sign up at Blogger. It takes hundreds of thousands of readers to earn anything approaching a living online.

That said, there are three well-known money-generating programs that are available to the average blogger.

Google AdSense (google.com/adsense). This program matches ads to your site's content. For instance, if you blog about travel, you might get ads from hotel booking services. If your readers click on these ads, then the hotel bookers pay Google, and Google pays you. Google is cagey about exactly how much you'll earn, in part because it's highly dependent on how much the advertisers pay Google. Suffice it to say you will get some portion of this amount.

Amazon Associates (amazon.com/associates). This is one of the web's oldest referral marketing programs. When you sign up,

Top Ten Horrible Publicity Stunt Ideas

1. Marry the top blogger in the blogroll and blog about it. Divorce one week later. Repeat on down the list.
2. Threaten to hold your breath until your counter hits ten thousand page views.
3. Pose as a labor and delivery nurse and snap first photos of the next Jolie-Pitt baby.
4. Try to erect a seventeen-ton popsicle in Times Square.*
5. Claim to be a teenager dying of cancer, blog about it, then have your "mom" blog about your death from a brain aneurysm.*
6. Start a rumor that a book based on your blog is the next Oprah selection (and, OMG, you're giving out tickets to the show where she'll discuss it!).
7. File a lawsuit claiming *Harry Potter and the Deathly Hallows* is suspiciously similar to Harry Potter fanfic you wrote on your blog.
8. Write the name of your blog in sprinkled baby powder on the Capitol's steps.
9. Write an open letter to the National Parks Service offering $10 million if they'll have the Statue of Liberty hold a sign with your blog name on it for a day (in place of the torch). Since you know they'll say no, it doesn't matter that you don't have $10 million.
10. Free gas! (Fine print: distributed by thimblefuls, must come to your house in Omaha to claim.)

*Actually happened.

Amazon gives you special links for your website that advertise Amazon and affiliates' products. When people click through and buy, you get a referral fee. This ranges from 4 percent on general products if you sell one to six items per month, to 8.5 percent if you sell more than 3,131 (the referral fee for high-priced products like computers is capped at a lower rate; some of Amazon's affiliates reimburse at higher rates). If you did manage to sell

3,131 $15 Amazon products in one month and got 8.5 percent for them, you'd make $3,992. Not bad for, say, running reviews of the books in question. But most people don't sell anywhere near 3,131 products—it's more likely you'll make enough to buy a book or two instead.

Yahoo! Publisher Network (publisher.yahoo.com). Like Google, Yahoo! is also in the business of selling ads online. As with Ad-Sense, you get paid when your readers click on ads on your site.

OTHER WAYS TO MAKE MONEY OFF YOUR BLOG

Running ads isn't the only way to turn blogging into an income-generating venture. There are a few other ways we've seen work:

Keep a blog for someone else. These days, corporations, foundations, and nonprofits are all using blogs to draw visitors to their sites. Some hire in-house bloggers, but others outsource this task to strong writers who are looking for extra (usually part-time) gigs.

Use your blog to build a platform for other ventures. Several bloggers have turned their online work into books (for which publishers pay advances; see *Stuff White People Like* or Shreve Stockton's *The Daily Coyote*). Some established writers use blogs to boost book sales. Other people use blogs to establish themselves as experts in a topic—either in order to give paid speeches about it or to sell something else. Denise Wakeman and Patsi Krakoff, who run the blog publicity company The Blog Squad, tell us that many of their small business clients use blogs to build buzz about their services. A man who packages golf tours to Asia, for instance, blogs constantly about updates in the worlds of golf and travel. People come for the content—and wind up booking expensive vacations while they're there.

Launch a new career. Good blog posts will show that you are a good writer. When editors ask you to show clips of your work, those first clips have to come from somewhere. A few well-written blog posts can serve as the basis for your portfolio. There are more tips in the next chapter on how to develop a compelling voice that makes people want to read your work again and again.

A BOY AND HIS BLOG

STEVEN WEBER, ACTOR AND HUFFPOST BLOGGER

I enjoy writing. I never said I was good at it. But evidently, people are gullible or just plain kind enough to read the things I write and mostly sprinkle modest praise upon me and my blog. I'll call my blog Rover.

Perhaps the worst thing about Rover (for me) is that I use it to fan the tiny sparks of my insecurity into ego-lapping flames of vanity. I admit that this is in many ways my raison d'être for being an actor, which is my primary method of employment. I'm not being humble, I'm being truthful. It also provides enjoyment in several other ways but I point it out because humility, I have learned, is attractive even when slightly pathetic, as that last admission certainly is. I love seeing my name in print (or in font, the electronic equivalent) as much as I like it if people recognize me from my acting. They are usually pleasant and rarely critical, at least to my face. Fun. Nice. Makes me feel good.

Rover, however, has changed that.

People fucking hate me. *Hate* me. They might have disliked me the way we all occasionally dislike an actor or actress. "Ew. I can't stand that actor/actress." But in my Rovers—

OK, I'll stop with this already lame comic device and just say my blogs—I never assume a character. I write my own dialogue (or rather, monologue). And I have done something no working actor should ever really do, which is reveal my political leanings and subsequently encourage a response other than praise from an audience.

What a schmuck. Again, not being humble. Being truthful. I am potentially biting the hand that feeds me and my family, not to mention transitioning me from the relative safety of being a happily middlebrow entertainer to being a pretentious would-be social commentator.

Surprisingly, I have enjoyed a fairly positive experience as a pretentious would-be social commentator. But I have also incurred the wrath of other would-be social commentators who might not share my political leanings and who grasp the lectern of their bully pulpit with the white-knuckled febrility of a bull rider on crystal meth. And not so much for these differing points of view but for my syntax. For my predilection for flowery phrasing. For my untethered grammar. That's like acting onstage wearing an Elizabethan doublet and hose and someone in the audience laughing maniacally at your crotch. It's low, it's unprofessional and insensitive, but that's what I get for stepping onto the boards with a misshapen crotch.

So essentially I have learned, as a blogger, to be truthful and humble, but to pay careful attention to the possibly labored technique of my little forays into social commentary, rather than worrying about offending people with the content. And to always wear a shapely yet inconspicuous codpiece. I wouldn't want to make any enemies.

CHAPTER 4

FINDING YOUR VOICE

Great bloggers all share one virtue in common:
They infuse their writing with a triple shot of
personality. Let your personality flow into
your blogging and your readers will find you.
—*Jeffrey Feldman, editor in chief of*
Frameshop and HuffPost blogger

his chapter is about writing. Specifically, it's about writing in a way that intrigues and persuades and that works with the unique format blogs allow. If you have bad memories of a teacher marking up your papers with a red pen, don't worry. What we want you to obsess about is finding your own voice and writing in a way that keeps your readers reading.

Like any craft, blogging has certain rules that good practitioners try to follow.

These rules are not carved in stone—and not just because there are eight of them and commandments come in batches of ten. "The question of what makes a blog post good is as simple and as complicated as asking what makes a poem beautiful, what makes a feature story captivating until the last line, what makes an essay persuasive, or what makes a novel force you to turn pages faster than you thought you ever could," says HuffPost associate blog

THE HUFFINGTON POST RULES FOR GREAT BLOGGING

1. Blog often
2. *Perfect* is the enemy of *done*
3. Write like you speak
4. Focus on specific details
5. Own your topic
6. Know your audience
7. Write short
8. Become part of the conversation with like-minded blogs

editor David Flumenbaum. Some writers are so brilliant that they can pull off anything. If Toni Morrison started a blog, she could write a stream-of-consciousness four-thousand-word rant once every six weeks, and you know what? We'd probably read it. When you win the Nobel Prize for literature, we'll read anything you write too. But until then, these rules will help keep you on track.

Rule # 1: Blog Often

If you're blogging for yourself, it doesn't matter how often you're writing. If you want an audience, though, you need to reward visitors to your site with new content—pretty much every time they visit. We've heard the arguments about quality vs. quantity, but we believe this argument is a luxury for people who've already got a big readership. When you don't have a reputation or a big following, you want people to judge you on the work you have produced. That means you need to have a lot of work sitting on your site by the time you start pulling in eyeballs. Plus, blogging is like anything else: You get better the more you do it. Writing often will help you figure out what your authentic voice sounds like and how you can access that voice every time you sit down to type. Definitions of "often" vary, but if you're serious about blogging, commit to posting at least two to three times a week for thirty days. As we learned from Ariane de Bonvoisin's blog, First 30Days, you can establish almost any new habit in one month's time. Mark on your calendar the days you plan to blog. Block off time in your appointment book. Then sit down and, to borrow a phrase from Nike, just do it.

Rule #2: *Perfect* Is the Enemy of *Done*

Because blogging is immediate, it's also informal—and that's a good thing. No hungover college student is going to study the perfect post alongside the great American novel. It's fine to write a bunch of OK posts. In fact, a bunch of OK posts is probably better than a perfect post that took so long to compose the event was old news by the time you hit "submit."

This is why some bloggers who are also professional writers love this genre. They find it immensely liberating.

Whenever you have a thought, you can share it with your readers. You can develop snippets of a story rather than crank out a five-thousand-word feature that the reader encounters only as a finished product. You get immediate feedback, which beats waiting three months for a magazine to appear on newsstands. And as much as we like editors, we do enjoy the ability to post in real time.

Still, we know that lots of bloggers suffer from writer's block.

Write as often as you possibly can. When I first started blogging, I would write one 500-to-1,200-word op-ed-style political analysis a day, five days a week. Coming up with good content—and insightful analysis—was certainly a challenge at that pace, but it meant I was getting exposure. Eventually, I scaled down to three days a week, but not until I had established myself.
—DYLAN LOEWE, FORMER EXECUTIVE DIRECTOR OF BATTLEGROUND, COLUMBIA LAW STUDENT, AND HUFFPOST BLOGGER

Weirdly, it's easier to blog every day than it is to blog three or four times a week. You get in a rhythm, you don't procrastinate, you load content into your blog, you loosen up, you'll be taken more seriously by readers, and you stay engaged with your subject and with what's happening on your blog.

—GRETCHEN RUBIN, AUTHOR OF THE HAPPINESS PROJECT BLOG AND HUFFPOST BLOGGER

Whenever we feel like banging our heads against the wall, we rely on a few shortcuts to create a perfectly adequate post.

The first shortcut? Just write a micropost on a small detail (see rule 4). Three to four sentences, in and out. How hard can that be? You can always post more later.

If you want to write more of an essay or op-ed post, here's a shortcut for that style:

- **What is your point?** How would you explain your point to a batty, slightly deaf relative in one sentence? Write that sentence down. This is the gist of your piece.
- Clear some space above that main point. Now think up a **story that illustrates the point.** This "anecdotal lede" is a staple of newspaper and magazine journalism. Reporters like anecdotes because they give a human-interest perspective on the story and tend to draw readers in. If the story happened to you, great. If you put in the proper links and cite the source, you can retell a story from another news source. You may have to write a transition sentence or two between the anecdote and your point.
- Now clear some space under your main point. Give a **short history of the debate.**
- Next, **argue your point from the evidence.** What makes you think you are right? Throw in two or three quotes, statistics, or stories that back you up.
- Now think about **who might disagree** with you. Why might this person or organization think you're wrong? Maybe it's because they're total idiots, but you'll write a better blog post if you address their strongest points rather than call them names.
- **Write a good walk-off line.** Or if you can't think of one,

write something like "I'll be following this story and will post again when I learn more."

Now proofread and double-check your facts. This last part is crucial. You can edit your post later if your facts turn out to be wrong (the blogospheric convention is to strike through the error so readers know a correction was made), but someone may have already read your mistake. The reader may have then cited your erroneous fact elsewhere—and that's how rumors get started. Pay close attention to names, numbers, and direct quotes. Screwing these up is just embarrassing. Once you're sure you're right, hit "submit." The post won't be perfect, but it will be done, and it will be accurate.

One final idea for those who really struggle with their inner critic: Try writing your thoughts longhand on an old-fashioned piece of paper that you know no one will see. Then, when you start typing, what appears on the screen will actually be a second draft.

Rule #3: Write Like You Speak

One of us recently had the experience of attending an academic symposium preceded by a dinner. At dinner, a fascinating, funny professor kept the whole table laughing through dessert. Everyone was looking forward to his speech. But once at the podium, he proceeded to read a dull, dense paper made bearable only by the fact that most of the audience was still buzzed from the wine.

Unfortunately, like the professor, too many of us have had the life beaten out of our prose through years of academic training and corporate PowerPoint presentations. We use big words when

Sources of Inspiration

So you're committed to blogging often with short, engaging (but not perfect) posts. Great! But what are you going to write about? Anything you feel passionate about. Here's our inspiration crib sheet.

1. **Newspapers.** Most bloggers read as many as possible—in print but mostly online (try linking to a hard copy paper and you'll see why).

2. **Political publications like *National Review* or *The Nation*.** If you lean left or right, read a publication with a different viewpoint. We bet you'll get riled up enough to write something.

3. **General interest publications.** Magazines like *Time, Newsweek, Vanity Fair, The New Yorker, Glamour, Men's Journal,* and *Sports Illustrated* all have fascinating features. Tear out a page to blog about later.

4. **TV news and news websites.** We get ideas while watching CNN on the treadmill. We also get ideas when the sweaty guy next to us switches (without asking!) to Fox News.

5. **Radio.** Maybe you listen to morning drive-time radio while you commute to work. Jot down an interesting tidbit while you're at a traffic light. Talk shows also make good fodder. Listen to a host whose opinions differ from yours, and answer his arguments.

6. **Large new-media sites.** HuffPost features hundreds of news stories and blog posts each day. You can also check out Politico, BoingBoing, Daily Kos, Gizmodo, Slate, Atlantic Online, Drudge, and other sites. You will never be short of information or topics to blog about.

7. **Blogs on your blogroll.** Link to their stories and discuss them on your own blog. Chances are, they'll soon do the same for you, whenever you come up with some original material.

8. **"On the street" reporting.** Are the teachers at your children's school upset by student test scores? Is the cafeteria manager concerned about the quality of the produce? Maybe your local pharmacist is worried that seniors don't understand recent changes in Medicare. All of these stories are worth covering.

More on Finding Inspiration

Probably my favorite blogging moment to date involves a piece I wrote for The Huffington Post titled "Hillary, O.J. and R.F.K.," about Hillary Clinton's now infamous [Robert F. Kennedy] assassination gaffe. I didn't initially intend to write about the incident but was inspired to do so after a conversation with a friend. She is really smart and engaged in the election and said that she thought Hillary's comment was "stupid" but also thought people were "overreacting" to it. She happens to be white and I'm African-American, and we ended up having this really interesting exchange about race and perception in the election. During our conversation I discovered that she had been completely unaware that many older African-Americans harbor very real fears about Barack Obama's safety. After our discussion she had a better understanding of where some of the reaction to Senator Clinton's comments came from. I realized in that moment that sometimes even between well-meaning, smart people, things simply get lost in translation. So I decided to write about this gaffe and why it struck such a chord among so many people—even if that was not the intention. After the piece appeared on The Huffington Post, I actually received a phone call from someone who had endorsed Senator Clinton who said that they felt the piece was one of the most honest, yet fair, assessments of the story they had read; yet I was also thanked by others for forcing a deeper conversation about our nation's somewhat tragic history as it pertains to the safety of prominent leaders of color, all of which made me feel really proud.

—KELI GOFF, AUTHOR OF *PARTY CRASHING: HOW THE HIP-HOP GENERATION DECLARED POLITICAL INDEPENDENCE* AND HUFFPOST BLOGGER

short ones will do. We use words that aren't really words, like *problematize*. Our sentences drag on far past their original intentions until some punctuation mark or another puts an end to the misery. We use adjectives and adverbs rather than nouns and verbs. We hide in the passive voice, as if evading responsibility for the mess that's been thrown up on the screen.

Most writing teachers have a simple cure for these ills: They'll tell you to go read William Strunk and E. B. White's classic, *The Elements of Style*. That's good advice. But if *The Huffington Post Complete Guide to Blogging* is the lone book you plan on reading this year, here's a tip that will improve your prose almost as much: Write like you speak.

The blogosphere thrives on authenticity. No one really sounds like a law paper, an academic paper, or a PowerPoint presentation. So your blog shouldn't sound like that either. You want your posts to sound like you at your most witty, entertaining, and relevant. Buy or borrow a small tape recorder. Tape yourself as you critique something you read in the newspaper. If you take out the "ums" and clean up the grammar, a transcription of this tape could be the start of a good post. Or don't clean up the grammar. On Rosie O'Donnell's Rosie.com blog, the actress and television per-

USE THE VOICE YOU HAVE
VERENA VON PFETTEN, LIVING EDITOR, HUFFINGTON POST

The best (and easiest) way to find your voice is to use the one you have. Sounds too easy? It's not. That's why blogging is so popular! First, think about blogging as writing an e-mail to a friend. Better yet, an e-mail to a really cool, clever friend with whom you have a great and witty rapport. (Don't have any cool, clever friends with whom you have a great and witty rapport? Make some new friends, then start blogging. Trust me, otherwise you won't have anyone to read your blog.) Second, just start writing. You don't spend hours hemming and hawing over how you're going to draft an e-mail, so don't spend hours hemming and hawing over a blog post. It's not worth the effort. Which brings me to my last point: Don't try too hard. Don't try to be funny (especially if you're not) and don't try to be serious (it's too much pressure). Don't try to be anything other than exactly who you are. It's your voice you're trying to find, after all.

sonality often just runs sentences together. Some people find that distracting and annoying, but judging by page views, it seems to be working for her.

Rule #4: Focus on Specific Details

Because blog posts are so immediate, and because there are so many blogs out there, you don't have to explain the complete context of an issue in every post, the way a newspaper or magazine story would. You don't have to fight for limited space the way a newspaper or magazine reporter would. In fact, your best bet for building buzz is to go into the specific, gory details and keep returning there.

Choose one nugget from a political speech or a proxy statement and blog about that. Do you think that $1.6 million is a little excessive for a security detail for a CEO that nobody can recognize anyway? Do you find it funny that a company that wants to be bought for $15 a share would pay an investment bank $15 million to tell everybody that yep, it's worth $15 a share? Write about a candidate's wife's cookie recipe. If you think something is news, post it. Don't wait to see if other people cover or keep covering the detail you found so interesting. If you've noticed that a columnist does consulting work for a company or interest group she just wrote about positively, get it out there.

Mainstream journalism tends to focus on conflict, rarities, and big trends. You can shape the narrative by focusing on the day-to-day—sometimes on the seemingly little things that get you riled up, sometimes on the view from your own backyard.

A Difference in Voice

Bloggers cover stories differently than the mainstream media does. Posts are more personal and informal than a page-one story. Here's an example: *The Wall Street Journal* excerpt is real. Farmer Bill is a total figment of our imaginations (underlined text in the blog example indicates a link).

The Wall Street Journal, page 1, July 1, 2008
Headline: Anger Rises over Salmonella Probe
Subhead: Tomato Investigation Stymies FDA, as Farmers, Distributors Face Mount-
    ing Losses
By Jane Zhang, Julie Jargon and A. J. Miranda

More than 11 weeks into a salmonella outbreak that has sickened hundreds across the U.S., government regulators still have little idea where the outbreak originated. That is causing rising anger among the farmers, distributors and others slammed by slumping sales of tomatoes, the outbreak's prime suspect . . .

Blog style: Farmer Bill (Florida)

Title: And we trust these guys to monitor our drugs?

Nearly three months after the FDA said tomatoes might be the cause of the latest salmonella outbreak, they're now saying they don't know for sure. Thanks, guys! Could you have mentioned this before my to-matoes died on the vine? (Thanks to all of you who have written asking if Barb and I are OK. We have savings. We'll get by.)

   I've just learned from John that Western Growers called for the House Agriculture Committee to inves-tigate the FDA's total boneheadedness on this issue. The National Restaurant Association says the out-break has cost the food industry some $100 million. And we still don't know where the contaminated tomatoes came from. Or if the problem is tomatoes. Now some people are saying jalapeño peppers are to blame.

   Oh, I know, the FDA is trying hard. They're busy. There's a lot of stuff going on up there. Like not ap-proving cancer drugs. (Thanks to Jen for the links on the FDA and the Provenge controversy.)

Rule #5: Own Your Topic

Mainstream reporters have "beats"—areas in which they're responsible for finding and breaking news. Likewise, if you want to be treated as an expert in your blog topic area, you should think of the topic as your beat. Know who the key players in that area are. Read their books. Interview them. Have them guest blog (that is, write a special post for you). Get copies of studies when they come out. E-mail the publicists for companies that sell products or services related to your area, introduce yourself, and ask to be put on press release distribution lists. Go to conferences. The more you know about your topic area, the better informed your opinions will be. This is important because a good blog errs on the side of being strong. Don't couch your voice in qualifiers. Writing is a risk. You're putting your ideas out there to see what will happen. Owning your topic area increases the chance that your ideas will be insightful and right.

Rule # 6: Know Your Audience

Blogs are interactive. After a while, you'll see which posts get the most comments and which wilt like untouched spinach on a picky eater's plate. It goes without saying that you should try to write more of the kinds of posts that get your readers excited and fewer posts that don't. Someday your public may love you so much that they'll eat their spinach if you tell them to. But why bank on it?

> I find that the blog posts that take the least amount of time
> turn out to be the most popular posts. I did one on what to
> wear when it's a hundred degrees outside, and everyone
> wanted to talk about that. But I can do twenty

CREATING "POLITICAL SPACE" AND CHANGING HISTORY

STEVEN CLEMONS, PUBLISHER OF THE WASHINGTON NOTE AND HUFFPOST BLOGGER

The Washington Note has broken numerous stories—but really my favorite involved starting the fight against John Bolton's confirmation as U.S. ambassador to the United Nations. My blog transformed itself from being a general-commentary political blog into one that was almost singularly obsessed for twenty-one months with the effort against Bolton's confirmation. I was at dinner with a foreign-policy expert when I heard news of George W. Bush's nomination of Bolton in March 2005—and I just couldn't believe it. I used to be the head of the Nixon Center in DC and thus am not an easy flack for the United Nations, but I couldn't imagine anything more destructive to America's place in the world via the United Nations than sending John Bolton there. Some of the key senators who didn't like Bolton told me that John Bolton was an obscure bureaucrat going for a job no one cared about—and that only if people like me created the "political space" would they be willing to do anything. So a number of us—triggered by some posts of mine on The Washington Note as well as some other smart thinking and dedicated work by key NGOs in Washington—took on Bolton and created that "political space." I ran into Karl Rove on a number of occasions during this time—once at the colonial-era liberal arts school on Maryland's eastern shore, Washington College. Rove told me at a reception, "Steve, we are going to get Bolton confirmed. We are going to check off that box." And I said, "No, not gonna happen. The Washington Note and its readers aren't just out around the country—they are senators and House members, intelligence and military officers, policy practitioners on the Hill and inside your own administration. They are Democrats, Republicans, and independents—and George Bush was wrong on this choice of our ambassador. He's going to lose." And Karl Rove and John Bolton did lose.

interviews, all this research, write a thoughtful post—
and get no comments.

*—Marci Alboher, Shifting Careers columnist
and blogger for* The New York Times

Rule #7: Write Short

We live in an ADD culture. Though you can write as much as you want on the web, we know from experience that unless the reader can see the end of your post eight hundred words in, a good portion of them will stop scrolling down. Even eight hundred words is an intimidating block of text. Break it up with a picture or pull quote, and definitely with some links. If you find that you can't do justice to your point in eight hundred to a thousand words, consider breaking the thought up into two or more posts. David Bromwich, a professor of English at Yale and HuffPost blogger says, "A good post is a single thought or observation or anecdote, clearly expressed and directly conveyed. An essay may cover several topics; a post easily grows tiresome if it aims for more than one."

We could go on about this, but you get our point. Readers will too if you keep it short.

Rule #8: Become Part of the Conversation with Like-Minded Blogs

The best writers learn from others. "You wouldn't try to make a movie if you'd never seen one," notes Katherine Goldstein, Huff-Post associate blog editor. So if you want to take your blog to the next level, spend some time scrutinizing posts from bloggers you admire. How do they draw you into their posts? How do they make their points? How do they find their stories? If you like a blog, post a comment saying so. E-mail the blogger and ask for a critique of some of your posts.

You should also ask your readers for their opinions. What do they like and dislike about your posts? What would they like to see more of?

It goes without saying that if you ask for comments and criticism, you should also be willing to offer feedback when asked. If a new blogger comes to you for advice, make time to give it. For starters, we all benefit from reflecting on what works and what doesn't. And second, you never know who will turn out to be the next Ana Marie Cox or Josh Marshall.

We'll discuss comments and the idea of building a community around your blog more in the next chapter.

FINDING A VOICE

JASON LINKINS, REPORTER, HUFFINGTON POST

I wish I could say that I was on the forefront of the blogging movement, but the truth is, I was a very late adopter. Which isn't to say I was late to the web itself. Long before blogging became popular, I was fascinated by the fresh perspective of web content and had put together my own website. Against the good advice of others, however, I remained resistant to blogging. There was just something about the format of blogging that didn't feel "pure" to me. I mean, how does the immediacy of blogging compare to the opportunity presented by four hours of hard coding in HTML? Or painstakingly updating multiple pages? Or archiving content by hand! Oh, yeah! That was probably the best of all!

As you might suspect, I had a moment where the scales finally fell from my eyes. For me, that moment came on Saturday, July 3, 2004, at a party in Washington DC's U Street neighborhood. It was there that I witnessed my friend, a grown man, in an attempt to demonstrate to his girlfriend that he loved her and would always be there for her, dress up in a tiger costume and leap through a ring of fire. Right then and there, I knew that everything had changed for me, because I walked away from the experience with the intense desire to tell the story of that evening to others. (My friend's girlfriend dumped him about a month later, which probably goes to show something. I know not what.)

I've made a handful of different attempts at blogging. Some were personal, some were conceptual. Some were successful, some were not. If there was a defining characteristic to the successful blogging I've done, it's the voice—that way of bridging the gap from brain to page. When I've felt comfortable with the voice of the blog, I've stuck with it. When it starts to feel fake to me, I quickly lose interest. There are many reasons for this: Obviously, good writing connects to a specific side of yourself that's stimulated by the thought of reaching other people. But blogging, and the way it encourages you to get your thoughts lined up in your mind and formed into words relatively quickly, can help reveal those aspects of language and writing that you love the most.

For me, I gravitated toward language that's punchy and rhythmic, analogies that challenged my observational skills, and long, satiric loops of logic. And, before long, I discovered that I could take my massive moral failings and countless personality defects and transform them into selling points. And somehow, in four short years, I went from blogging about tiger costumes to writing full-time about politics for The Huffington Post. Could the same amazing upward climb happen for you?

Probably not! Still, blogging regularly can breed that spark of voice—and its evolution—and like a new operating system for your mind, the constant return to the exercise of writing breeds a greater capacity for expressing your ideas sensibly and relatably. This was, to me, the practical demonstration of an idea I once expressed to one of my English professors—that if reading expanded the heart of one's intellect, the practice of writing provided the intellect with tone and definition. "And if you know what's good for you," my professor said, "you will get the hell off of my front yard before I call the police."

And I did so, quickly. Because, man, I did not need that hassle.

CHAPTER 5

COMMUNITY: CREATING AND BUILDING IT

As we advance in the Internet era, the reasons people go online have changed. In the late 1990s, we thought everyone would want to e-mail, shop for pet food, or read whatever information a company or organization chose to put on its home page. Media outlets created websites to expand their readership, but they basically uploaded their daily print content—nothing more and nothing less.

It's become fashionable to refer to this mind-set retroactively as Web 1.0. Now we're deep into Web 2.0. It's a buzzword that means different things to different people, but the gist is this: When people go online these days, they want to be able to interact with the people and content they find there. As they interact, they create communities that are united by like interests or temperaments. These communities don't have to suffer from the limits that differences in geography, race, sex, age, appearance, or class have put on us in the past. You, a mom in New York, can converse for years with a mom from Illinois whom you've never actually "met." But when she has to put her cat to sleep, you will send reams of sympathy e-mails. We've heard plenty of stories of

THE BLOGOSPHERE: AN INSTANTANEOUS, RAUCOUS DEMOCRACY

DEEPAK CHOPRA, BESTSELLING AUTHOR AND HUFFPOST BLOGGER

The blogosphere produces conflict in a writer. It's a raucous democracy, a global Athens with all kinds of customers striding through the agora. Perverse thoughts intermingle with healthy ones, like bacteria and vaccine in the same syringe. Vituperative cowards snipe from the safety of an anonymous keyboard. Walking psychotics effloresce their symptoms. Yet the temptation is to return again and again. Not simply to be heard (the fraction of words actually listened to must be less than a glass of water in the Niagara), not simply for the freak show, not even for the liveliness of the debate. More than these, a writer is motivated because the blogosphere is instantaneous. Every opinion is fresh off the shelf, and there's a unique thrill in broadcasting your brain, minute by minute, across the world. Of course that's mostly a fantasy, but so is every other means of communication. Talking person to person, one can be totally misunderstood, just as on the Net. Blogs give you a chance to be misunderstood en masse—and grateful when that one sympathetic reader responds and gives you hope for the future of the mind.

people isolated by illness who find new life as the wittiest poster on, say, a current affairs blog.

This chapter is about building the kind of community around your blog that makes the blogosphere a fascinating—and sometimes even warm and fuzzy—place to be. "A blog is only as good as the people who read it," says Katie Saddlemire, HuffPost's community manager. That is why one of your top priorities as a blogger should be to make your readers feel loved. The best way to do this is through prudent management of the comments feature. "Comments have their downsides, but if managed well, you can use them to create a space for lively debate that keeps readers

WHY WE NEED ANONYMOUS COMMENTERS

JOHN RIDLEY, NOVELIST, SCREENWRITER, AND HUFFPOST BLOGGER

A constant of nature is that with substantive progress comes useless by-product. With fire, there is ash. With nuclear power, there is nuclear waste. With television, there is *Two and a Half Men*. This universal constant is equally true with blogging. That which has allowed for the unfiltered expression of the reasoned, the informed, and the thoughtful has also disgorged that which is the anonymous responder. This is not meant in any way to denigrate the essential value of the anonymous responder. The same as carbon monoxide, they, the nameless, are part of the gaseous composition that drives the engine of the digital age. Without the unsigned masses who are compelled at odd hours to respond to anything and everything posted on the web, bloggers would merely be Internet writers—which is just the unemployed version of mainstream media journalists.

coming back for more," she says. "That's what we like to do at HuffPost."

So far, it seems to be going pretty well. Our bloggers often tell us that the sheer volume of comments they get at HuffPost keeps them posting. With over 260,000 registered members, we sometimes get as many as 20,000 comments per day. Lots of comments means lots of people are reading, "and that is immensely rewarding for any writer," says Jim Moore, an Emmy-winning TV news correspondent and HuffPost blogger. "I have written pieces for major publications like the *Los Angeles Times* and *The Boston Globe* and the *Financial Times* and I am quite confident none of them were as carefully read or as widely read as my blogs on Huff-Post." A Site Meter counter can tell you that people are reading your blog. But only comments can tell you that they care.

Of course, "care" doesn't necessarily mean "agree with you."

Like an honest friend, a good blog community will tell you when you've got toilet paper trailing from your shoe.

"The interactivity from commenters is a gift and a curse," says Spencer Ackerman, a senior reporter at The Washington Independent and HuffPost blogger. "I like hearing critiques of my work, and I like getting suggestions and ideas for other stuff I should cover, but there's only so many times a day you can read about how much you suck. I suppose you shouldn't play with fire if you're not prepared to see the burn ward, though." Some bloggers describe their rougher days as requiring "Teflon underwear" to keep from sustaining flame war injuries.

But while blogging requires a tough skin, it need not require special Skivvies. This chapter tells you how to build a blog community that resembles a campfire—with lots of singing and telling stories—rather than a bunch of arsonists trying to burn each others' houses down. We'll end this chapter with a short discussion of the broader blogging community, including its awards and in-person institutions.

Best Practices for Building Community

These guidelines will help create a sense of inclusion around your blog and keep thoughtful readers coming back:

- **Create clear community guidelines**
- **Ask readers for input**
- **Read and respond to your comments**
- **Rate and reward good comments**
- **Keep the conversation going**
- **Make yourself accessible**
- **Admit when you are wrong**
- **Nix spam**
- **Keep people in line**

The first seven of these guidelines are about being the good cop who gets to know the kids on the block. You hand out candy for good grades and fill in as a referee in the local soccer game. The last two are a bit more "bad cop," cracking down on the kid who breaks windows before he goes out and breaks someone's head. All are necessary to create the kind of neighborhood a normal person would want to live in.

Create clear community guidelines. As Saddlemire puts it, "People appreciate knowing what to expect. If you expect readers to comment on your blog, it's a good idea to create a set of simple ground rules for them to follow." Include basic information in your guidelines, such as what your blog is about. What is not OK

Your voice should be engaging. Invite reader commentary and criticism, and respond to it. Develop a tone that encourages others to speak their mind, and listen to them. Allow them to help you get better.
—ALEXANDER REMINGTON, *THE WASHINGTON POST* EDITORIAL ASSISTANT AND HUFFPOST BLOGGER

for people to say? Under what circumstance will you delete a comment? "Being up front about your standards helps keep things civil and gives you something to point to when someone breaks the rules," Saddlemire says. You can read HuffPost's guidelines later in this chapter on page 105.

Ask readers for input. End posts with some version of "what do you think?" or ask for people's personal experiences with the issue you're writing about. In 2006 and again in 2008 HuffPost won a Webby Award for Best Political Blog. One of the fun things about the Webbys is that winners must limit their acceptance speech to five words. So both times Arianna asked HuffPost readers for their suggestions. In 2006, our commenters offered up over 300 five-word speeches. "Our HuffPost team kept going back and forth over dinner as to which one I should use," Arianna recounted in her blog the day after the Awards. "Among the top contenders proposed by our readers: 'It's all Geek to me,' 'So, missions CAN be accomplished!,' 'Couldn't do it without Bush,' and 'The WMD are located at . . . ' And our editor, Roy Sekoff, came up with two that remained in the running right until I walked on stage: 'W's not the only decider' and 'The revolution will be blogged.'

"In the end, I ended up going with the five-word speech offered by HuffPost commenter simonw, with me adding a little self-mocking twist: 'Dah-lings,' I said, ratcheting up the accent, 'Make blogs, not war.' I considered going with 'Make blogs, not fucked-up wars,' but cooler heads—i.e., my partner Kenny Lerer— prevailed. So thanks to simonw; if you're ever in New York, stop by the office and borrow the Webby for as long as you like."

In 2008, our readers came through with what Arianna called "an embarrassment of pithy riches—offering up over 1,000 suggestions. Some were impassioned, some were funny, many were both—and all were very creative. Color us impressed. And appreciative: Thanks to everyone who sent one in.

"It was a very tough call but, in the end, we decided to go with 'President Obama . . . Sounds good, right?,' submitted by Sunflower1. The other finalists were: 'Big Brother, *we're* watching *you*' (submitted by SilthyTove); 'No country for old media' (jungpatawan); and 'Fuck it . . . We'll liveblog it!' (LiarLiarIraqsOnFire)"

One thing: if you ask for input, you should be prepared to . . .

Read and respond to your comments. If a poster has directly addressed you or brought up a thoughtful critique of your idea, you should answer this comment. If for some reason you don't think your answer should be public, try to e-mail the person, or ask the person (in the comments section) to e-mail you. This indicates to other posters that you have registered the comment. Note: You should make it clear that you, the blogger, are the person responding (see the Lee Siegel story below).

Rate comments and reward the good ones. Some blogging programs have a feature allowing you to recommend a comment. People often put a lot of effort into their comments. Logan Nakyanzi Pollard, executive producer of Air America Radio and HuffPost blogger, posted an essay not too long ago called "Oh I Get It, the Left Just Doesn't Want to Win This Year." It got over six hundred comments, but "what surprised me more than the number of responses was the level of engagement the readers were making with the post," he says. "Folks were writing their own essays to answer mine, and then posting even more commentary in response to other readers' reactions." Good posts deserve

Don't be put off by some of the comments that seem negative or even hostile. Some provide interesting criticisms, and we learn more from criticism than from praise, pleasant though the latter may be.

—JOSEPH NYE, PROFESSOR OF INTERNATIONAL RELATIONS AT HARVARD UNIVERSITY AND HUFFPOST BLOGGER a bump. Over time, people who consistently post good comments can achieve celebrity status at a site. Make a point of noting the good ones—you might invite these readers to guest blog from time to time. Not only will this make them feel ever more that they're a part of your community, it will buy you a well-deserved vacation.

Keep the conversation going. Sometimes a thoughtful post can spark a whole new round of deliberation. Write posts that reply to what's being said in the comments. Posts based on comments send the unmistakable message that you care about what readers think.

Make yourself accessible outside of the comments section. Post an e-mail address where readers can send tips, praise, or critiques. Thank people who've bothered to send you thoughtful e-mails, and respond to any legitimate beefs (like complaints about your horrible background template).

Admit when you are wrong. You should double- and triple-check your facts. But if you make a mistake or new information comes to light, a growing convention in the blogosphere is to correct a post using the strike-through feature to make changes so readers can see what you said originally and see the correction right next to it. The golden rule of community is to treat other people how you would like to be treated—and no one wants to hang out with someone who refuses to acknowledge when they've stepped in it.

If comment threads lead into areas about which
your knowledge is incomplete, readers will respect

your willingness to say the most important three
words in the English language: "I don't know."
—*Todd Seavey, Facts and Fears for the
American Council on Science and Health blog*

Nix spam. Though thousands of new spam blogs are started every day, some spammers aren't content to stick to their own blogs. They want to put ads on yours. Their bots crawl through cyberspace posting links to penile enhancement pills and gold speculation schemes on any unprotected blog they can find. These posts are annoying both to you ("Wow, six comments! Oh, wait . . .") and to your readers, who have to skip over them to get to the red meat of the debate. Many blogging software programs have anti-spam features. A popular one requires readers to type in CAPTCHAs (which stand for "Completely Automated Public Turing Test to tell Computers and Humans Apart") when they submit a comment or post. CAPTCHAs are usually weird-looking letters and/or numbers. A human can recognize that a squiggly Q is still a Q (unless you have bad eyesight; good programs have different options for the visually impaired). A computer has more difficulty with this task. Consequently, posts that make it through this screen were most likely created by humans, and actual human beings tend to get bored typing posts about penile enhancement all day.

It's not foolproof. Not long ago, one spammer devised a scheme that had humans solving CAPTCHAs in order to look at pornographic images. As each CAPTCHA was solved, spam got through site filters. But it works pretty well and, more importantly, CAPTCHAs aren't a big enough deterrent to keep most legitimate posters from having their say.

Keep people in line. This is a section unto itself. It is part of the larger question of whether bloggers should moderate their comments, and if they do, whether they should do it proactively or after the fact. By proactively, we mean reading and evaluating each comment before it sees the light of day on your blog. Most of the major blogging software programs have a moderating feature that allows you to do this. When you switch on the moderating feature, the software e-mails you (or otherwise alerts you) every time someone posts a comment. You decide whether to accept or delete the comment.

The question of whether to pre-moderate depends on both your blog size and your tolerance for the odder life forms of the blogosphere.

If you have a relatively small blog with only one or two posts a day and a few dozen comments at most, you probably don't need to pre-moderate. Horrible posts will be rare enough that you can deal with them after the fact. "You want to read through the comments that are posted to your site and address any that violate your rules," Katie Saddlemire, our community manager, says. "Some bloggers delete bad comments, some post replies reminding everyone of their rules. A lot of blog software has ways for you to ban users from commenting, which can be useful for repeat offenders. Do what you're comfortable doing, and be consistent."

This idea of moderating after the fact on small blogs is not a hard and fast rule. If your blog deals with a sensitive subject, you might draw more nastiness than you would otherwise. Joan Price, who keeps a blog about sex after age sixty called Better Than I Ever Expected (and is the author of a book by the same name), tells us that "a couple of radio 'shock jocks' ridiculed my blog and invited their readers to visit it and comment." When she stopped by later, "my blog was peppered with horribly vile and obscene comments. It took me a whole morning to find and delete all of them." So now she keeps the moderating feature turned on. She reads comments and either accepts them or deletes them.

Of course, if you are your blog's sole "employee," pre-moderating has downsides. You have to remember to check your site, or check

We never censor comments based on political or ideological point of view. We only delete those comments that . . .

- are abusive, off-topic, or use excessive foul language
- use ad hominem attacks, including comments that celebrate the death or illness of any person, public figure or otherwise
- contain racist, sexist, homophobic, or any other slurs
- are solicitations and/or advertising for personal blogs and websites
- use thread spamming (you've posted this same comment elsewhere on the site)
- are posted with the explicit intention of provoking other commenters or the staff at The Huffington Post.

your e-mail for pending comments, as often as you can. Legitimate readers get annoyed when they have to wait a week for a comment to appear. At that pace, they may as well write their newspaper a letter to the editor! You have to give up a lot of spontaneity to deal with bullying incidents this way.

Larger blogs, on the other hand, can have multimillion-person audiences. That sometimes brings out the kinds of people who enjoy the virtual equivalent of streaking at the Super Bowl. So sites like ours do monitor all comments before they're posted. We actually have over two dozen people who spend their time monitoring HuffPost comments (they work remotely, though sometimes we like to picture a war room of moderators zapping nuclear comments as they come in).

We think of pre-moderation as akin to stopping a nutcase from shouting "fire" in a crowded comedy club so everyone else can enjoy Bill Maher in peace.

The above guidelines, unheeded, would make HuffPost a less pleasant place for the 99 percent of site visitors who visit us for the right reasons. We don't believe we—or you—have any responsibility to establish a platform for the 1 percent of visitors who are "trolls" (Internet slang for disrupters intent on mischief). You know who these people are—the ones who post on a progressive site that all Democrats are pedophiles, or on a conservative site that all Republicans are Nazis, or on a site celebrating tulips that tulips should be ground up and incorporated into bathroom tile. Their whole purpose in posting is to sow discord and get attention (because their own blogs probably aren't getting any).

But we want to stress that trolls are part of the negative fringe—not the rule—of the blogosphere. This is where we differ from cultural critic Lee Siegel, who became the poster child for troll behavior two years ago, even though he frequently rails against it.

A writer for *Slate, The Nation,* and other places, Siegel joined the staff of *The New Republic* in June 2006 as a senior editor. He started keeping a blog on the website. As often happens, readers left anonymous comments in the magazine's "TalkBack" section criticizing his work. In particular, some fans of *The Daily Show* host Jon Stewart took issue with Siegel's criticism of the comedian.

In response, Siegel decided to create a virtual sock puppet who would defend him and savage his critics. He called this character "sprezzatura." The *New Republic* user sprezzatura proceeded to praise Siegel mightily on the boards and even told other readers that "Siegel is brave, brilliant, and wittier than Stewart will ever be. Take that, you bunch of immature, abusive sheep."

You can see where this is going. When *The New Republic* figured out why sprezzatura was so passionate, the magazine decided that creating multiple electronic personalities to insult the readership was poor form. *TNR* suspended Siegel in September 2006, though—making this less of a morality tale—he had resumed writing by April 2007. He also got a book contract out of the deal. His *Against the Machine: Being Human in the Age of the Electronic Mob* came out in January 2008. In it, he blasts the Internet, "where the rhetoric of democracy, freedom, and access is often a fig leaf for antidemocratic and coercive rhetoric; where commercial ambitions dress up in the sheep's clothing of humanistic values; and where, ironically, technology has turned back the clock from disinterested enjoyment of high and popular art to a primitive culture of crude, grasping self-interest."

Well . . .

To be fair, some of our own bloggers also note that the Internet's anonymity can do strange things to people. "If you're writing on a hot topic, the mob mentality can and will emerge," says Beth Arnold, a journalist and HuffPost blogger. "Get ready for attacks, because they'll come. For the most part, it doesn't bother me for people to passionately disagree because I like the debate spirit. But I have been astonished at how vicious and mean people can be over any subject. You wouldn't want to meet some of them on the street. You wouldn't want them to know your address or phone number. When the mob mentality sits down at the table, you feel the rage that lies under the surface of humanity and the social constructs of civilization."

We certainly have seen some comment threads get nasty. We've seen them hijacked and seen people get ganged up on. But no one who's attended a condo board meeting thinks this facet of human nature is unique to the anonymous world of the Internet. What is unique to the Internet is its ability to create a real-time conversation between people who might never have the opportunity to meet each other in person because they can't afford the same condos in the first place. We've seen some incredibly thoughtful comments. We've seen witty comments. Of course, two pitchfork-wielding mob members might still have time for witty repartee on their way to burn a few witches. But not all in-person interactions are brilliant or meaningful either. What matters is the ratio. And frankly, we're having a lot more discussions about democracy, human values, and the like these days than we did fifteen years ago.

All this is to say that, while the blogosphere can be a wild place, camp counselors and the conscientious kids who are appalled at such things usually stop fights before too much marshmallow ends up in people's hair. As a blogger, it's your responsibility to deal with the handful of people who like flame wars, so everyone else will enjoy the campfire, the conversation, and the debate.

Community Institutions

"I'd like to thank the Academy . . ."

Like any other creative community, the blogosphere touts those who practice the craft well. People do this every day with links, but sometimes it's fun to put on a virtual red-carpet show. Blog awards are a lot like blogs themselves. Anyone can start one. Some awards garner far more nominations and votes than others. Winning is often based on turnout (so if you want to win an award, find an unknown one, then badger all your readers to vote). Here are a few we've come across.

The Webby Awards (www.webbyawards.com). These honor all kinds of Internet properties, of which blogs are one. Established in 1996, the Webbys are presented by The International Academy of Digital Arts and Sciences whose members include David

Bowie, Matt Groening, Richard Branson, Harvey Weinstein, and Arianna Huffington. Winners must limit their acceptance speech to five words. HuffPost has won twice for Best Political Blog, in 2006 and 2008.

The "Bloggies" (bloggies.com). You won't get much cash (2008 prizes for the biggest categories were 2008 cents, or $20.08) but the scope of categories is impressive. Fat Cyclist (from a cyclist named Elden whose wife is fighting breast cancer) won the best sports blog in 2008, and we found ourselves strangely sucked into the Best African Blog, Dotty Rhino, about a rhino named Dotty's adventures in the Mkomazi Game Reserve in Tanzania.

Blogger's Choice Awards (bloggerschoiceawards.com). Run by IZEA, a social media marketing company. Winners in 2007 included Rosie.com for the best celebrity blog and Slope of Hope—about U.S. stock charts—as a top business blog.

The Blooker Prize (lulublookerprize.typepad.com). With a nod at the esteemed Man Booker Prize (for books), self-publishing outlet Lulu.com gave the Lulu Blooker for the best book based on a blog in 2006; the contest subsequently continued as the Blooker Prize in 2007. Winners in 2006 included Julie Powell's *Julie and Julia: 365 Days, 524 Recipes, 1 Tiny Apartment Kitchen*, her memoir of cooking through Julia Child's *Mastering the Art of French Cooking, Volume I*. The top winner in 2007 was *My War: Killing Time in Iraq* by Colby Buzzell (Arianna Huffington was a judge).

The Best of Blog Awards (thebestofblogs.com). This competition finds some lesser-known gems. Categories include, among many others, Best Health/Fitness Blog (2008 winner: Escape from Obesity), Best Mommy Blog (Punk Rock Mommy), Best Homeschooling/Education Blog (a runner-up was named, intriguingly, Three Standard Deviations to the Left), and best sports blog (I'll Run for Donuts, from a blogger whose hobbies are, in fact, running and donuts).

"In Real Life" Blogging Communities

Blogs are part of a virtual community, but sometimes people like to put a face to a screen name and maybe change out of their pajamas for a while.

One way to **meet other bloggers is at the BlogWorld and New Media Expo.** This annual event attracts everyone from bloggers themselves to companies that serve bloggers and companies that advertise on blogs. There's also the occasional celebrity (Dallas Mavericks owner Mark Cuban was the 2007 keynote speaker).

Another way to meet bloggers is through **Meetup groups.** The website Meetup.com helps people find other like-minded folks to hang out with in person. Sample blogging groups include Bay Area Bloggers (405 members when we checked) and BKLN 2.0 (308 members).

Still, these Meetup numbers are awfully low given the actual number of Bay Area or Brooklyn bloggers. So if you'd like to meet other bloggers in person, your best bet is to create your own group. (In moments of fancy, we envision these "blogging circles" to be like the sewing circles of the past. A few people would gather with their laptops, Wi-Fi, and a few glasses of wine and post about life . . .)

When you find another blogger you admire—and you become a regular member of that blog's community—check the person's profile to see if a city is listed. If so, and you're planning on visiting the city at some point, send a note saying you'll be in town. Ask for something harmless like restaurant recommendations. Chances are, the person will ask if you want to get together. If another blogger e-mails you, consider meeting that blogger in person as well. Choose somewhere public and busy—but you're far more likely to meet a friend than an ax murderer. Join blog networks or form your own. If you're part of a network of New York mom bloggers, for instance, you can host a picnic in Central Park. Or if you become well known enough, you can start giving

HOW BLOGGING IS REVOLUTIONIZING AMERICAN DEMOCRACY

JEFFREY FELDMAN, EDITOR IN CHIEF OF FRAMESHOP AND HUFFPOST BLOGGER

In July 2005 I led a Democracy Fest workshop under a tent on a brutal Texas summer day—the first time I stood in front of a group of people who had come to see me solely because of my writing as a blogger. While it was hot enough to fry an egg, the audience and I connected from first word to last—over an hour of analytical discussion about the place of persuasive language in American politics, a topic difficult to get through in perfect conditions, let alone when the thermometer tops a hundred degrees in the shade. It was a watershed moment for me. The bond that I had with that group without ever having met one of them was a product of the interaction between reader and writer that happens on blogs. It was on that hot Texas morning that I realized how revolutionary blogging was for American democracy and for the lives of everyone in it. Much more than citizen journalism, blogging catalyzes community, rapidly rebuilds the ties between people, and recenters our nation on the people that give it meaning. I believe every blogger has a story like mine, whether in Texas or in Tennessee, with ten people or with ten thousand. It is the moment when we feel our blogging come to life in the faces, voices, and hearts of people.

speeches and hosting meetings that will catalyze your readers to work together on the issues you address.

In the past, our conversations—and our attempts to learn from and understand each other—were mostly limited to the people in our immediate lives. Blogging helps us extend our sphere of influence. It also broadens the community of people we can learn from. Because of this dizzying scope, we're not worried that Americans are spending too much time hiding in dark rooms with computers, insulting each other anonymously. Yes, some people are doing this. But most of us choose to take advantage of the new social possibilities blogs provide. Far from being isolated cranks, we're building bigger communities than ever before.

In the next section, we'll share how HuffPost got started, its impact, and how your blog can be a part of this revolution in communicating and relating.

PART II

THE BLOG REVOLUTION IS HERE! BE A PART OF IT.

THE IMPACT OF THE HUFFINGTON POST AND OTHER BLOGS—AND HOW MAINSTREAM MEDIA WILL NEVER BE THE SAME.

CHAPTER 6

A BLOG IS BORN:
A BRIEF HISTORY OF
THE HUFFINGTON POST
AND ITS IMPACT

The first whisperings of what would become The Huffington Post started shortly after November 2, 2004. Those of us who were around at the beginning—like many progressives—woke up after the 2004 election wondering what the hell happened. Bush had actually lost the popular vote four years earlier and hadn't done much to expand his coalition since then. So when Bush pulled it out again and won—and Republicans retained control of Congress—the conversation at political gatherings and parties turned to what went wrong.

One of the problems was the way the mainstream media had spent 2004 obsessed with the horse race of the election—e.g., what effect the Swift Boat Veterans for Truth ads would have on Kerry's poll numbers, rather than whether the ads were accurate or why they were being aired in the first place.

Enter Arianna Huffington, author and syndicated columnist, and Kenny Lerer, a former AOL executive. Arianna has always been what business writer Malcolm Gladwell calls a "connector"— that is, someone who knows everyone and enjoys finding ways

A PIONEERING BRIDGE

GARY HART, FORMER U.S. SENATOR AND HUFFPOST BLOGGER

By offering a wide range of news, information, and opinions on the events of the day, The Huffington Post represents a pioneering bridge from the old media to the new. Years, if not months, from now, those observing this historic transition will credit The Huffington Post with seeing the media future more clearly than anyone else and with building a platform for informing the public, and particularly the younger public, of the future. As a member of a generation passing from the public stage, the Huffington blogosphere has provided me a venue for my own idiosyncratic opinions available nowhere else.

to bring them together. She and Kenny had been introduced by Tom and Kathy Freston and had become good friends. Over the course of many conversations in the lead-up to the election and its aftermath, they talked about the need for a new kind of site that incorporated aggregated news and the powerful force of blogging that was starting to flex its muscles at the time. Wouldn't it be fascinating, they thought, to take the conversations, the ideas, the debate, and the excitement of one of Arianna's gatherings and put it online alongside a progressive version of what Matt Drudge was doing with news aggregation?

Arianna and Kenny tapped their Rolodexes to figure out the feasibility of such a project. Arianna brought in Roy Sekoff, a screenwriter who'd worked as a writer/correspondent on Michael Moore's Emmy-winning *TV Nation* and had teamed with Arianna on a number of projects, including the 2000 Shadow Conventions she organized to address the issues neither political party was addressing. Kenny brought in Jonah Peretti, a young viral-marketing visionary. They also tapped Andrew Breitbart, who had worked on

JONAH PERETTI | BIO

The Huffington Post is live!

Posted May 9, 2005 | 03:32 AM (EST)

Read More: Breaking Home News

Let the madness begin.

Email ▶   Print ▶

creating Arianna's personal website, ariannaonline.com, and who worked with Drudge and was hence a veteran of the online news game.

By late February 2005, the gang of five signed on to make this new "Huffington Post" a reality. All that had to happen was, well, just about everything.

No one had built a big-name group blog before. Arianna, Kenny, and crew spent twelve weeks before launch hashing out every detail. Should the group blog be on the left or the right of the page? (Left.) More importantly, should the editors maintain control of what blog posts were featured on the home page, or should they allow new posts to automatically appear, bumping each old post down as it did? (Editorial control.)

Andrew and Roy sat in Arianna's house, sketching the raw layout of the site on a scrap of paper (alas, not an actual napkin). Coders—led by Andy Yaco-Mink—tried to turn these sketches into reality. Mena and Ben Trott, the founders of Six Apart (which produces Movable Type, the software that powers HuffPost), flew in and, over dinner at Arianna's house, began to figure out how they could expand their platform for effective group blogging. Magazine illustrator R. O. Blechman designed a simple but elegant template.

There was also much discussion about the appropriate attitude for this new site. We kept coming back to the idea of "branded content." That is, we wanted readers to be able to tell, without any signage, that they were reading HuffPost fare. We also wanted to show that while we took what we were doing very seriously, we didn't take ourselves seriously. During a brainstorming session, Arianna and Roy landed on a tagline for the site that captured this approach: "The Huffington Post: Delivering News and Opinion Since May 9, 2005"—i.e., roughly five minutes prior. The Old Gray Lady this was not.

As the infrastructure was being built, Arianna turned her attention to the content that would appear on the site. She approached her network of friends and asked them to blog. A host of boldface names quickly signed on, including Nora Ephron, Larry David, Bobby Kennedy Jr., Bill Maher, Harry Shearer, Arthur Schlesinger Jr., Gary Hart, Norman Lear, Walter Cronkite, John Cusack, David Mamet, Vernon Jordan, Tina Brown, Jann Wenner, Laurie David, Harry Evans, Julia Louis-Dreyfus, Brad Hall, Ari Emanuel, Paul Reiser, Andy Stern, and Adam McKay.

By late April, HuffPost went into labor-intensive beta-testing. The first bloggers started sending in content. On May 8, 2005, the day before launch, the HuffPost team worked for nearly twenty-four hours straight loading posts, along with blogger bios

and photos. We went live in the middle of the night in case anything went horribly wrong.

It didn't. In fact, as launches go, ours was remarkably charmed.
AOL linked to the site. *The New York Times* gave it a nice write-up.
The editors of *New York* magazine had a lunch where Arianna
walked them through the site. Charlie Rose interviewed Arianna
about HuffPost on his PBS show. Nothing technical exploded.

That's not to say everyone was thrilled. Nikki Finke slammed
HuffPost in *LA Weekly* (she called the blog "such a bomb that it's
the movie equivalent of *Gigli, Ishtar,* and *Heaven's Gate* rolled into
one"). Others worried the site would be little more than celebrity
blather. But intellectuals like Arthur Schlesinger Jr. helped anchor
the content, and many of the Hollywood-type contributors turned
out to have a lot to add to the national conversation.

Many found it addictive from the start.

Larry David dictated his first blog post, "Why I Support John
Bolton," via phone from the set of *Curb Your Enthusiasm.* "I know
this may not sound politically correct," he wrote, "but as someone
who has abused and tormented employees and underlings for
years, I am dismayed by all of this yammering directed at John
Bolton . . . Let's face it, the people who are screaming the loudest
at Bolton have never been a boss and have no idea what it's like to
deal with nitwits as dumb as themselves all day long." Ever the
perfectionist, he called back multiple times to tweak, polish, edit,
and hone his post.

Pulitzer Prize–winning playwright David Mamet promised
Arianna he'd blog but didn't appear overly excited by the concept.
He titled his launch-day post "This Computer Thing." In it he
declared, "I understand that computers, which I once believed to
be but a hermaphrodite typewriter–cum–filing cabinet, offer the
cyber-literate increased ability to communicate," only to then pre-

dict that these "computer 'blogs'" would soon be "as little deserving of our trust as are the books, journals, films, broadcasts, dramas, and flyers upon which we already depend for that we have come, in our need, to applaud as 'information.'" Then, just three days after that first post, *New York* magazine fired its dyspeptic theater critic, John Simon, a longtime Mamet nemesis. And Mamet couldn't resist the desire to blog about it. On May 12, he e-mailed this post to Arianna: "I have just heard that John Simon has been fired from the post he long disgraced at *New York* magazine. In his departure he accomplishes that which during his tenure eluded him: he has finally done something for the American theatre." Mamet later decided to try a new genre of creative expression and was soon hand-delivering cartoons to Arianna's house. We couldn't post them fast enough.

Norman Mailer also wasn't sure he wanted to blog. He had a book in the works—could we call back in a few years? Then stories that U.S. interrogators had flushed a copy of the Koran at Guantánamo Bay hit the news, triggering days of deadly rioting in Afghanistan. Mailer had a take on it and wanted it published quickly. "I'm beginning to see why one would want to write a blog," he wrote, opening a post claiming that *Newsweek*'s big scoop, and subsequent retraction, was "redolent with bad odor." By the time of his second post, he was getting into the spirit of blogging in his own inimitable way: "The following is just for the sake of it—I want to feed the maw of the blog."

Nora Ephron blogged for the first time during our first month, when Mark Felt revealed his identity as Watergate's "Deep Throat" (as Carl Bernstein's ex-wife, it was a subject close to her heart). "For many years I have lived with the secret of Deep Throat's identity," she wrote. "It has been hell, and I have dealt with the situation by telling pretty much anyone who asked me, including total strangers, who Deep Throat was. Not for nothing is indiscretion my middle name." Her post flew around the Internet—and into the mainstream media—from the moment she hit "publish."

Ephron's humor is a big draw for HuffPost, which has been blessed with many who have serious comedic chops. Comedy headliners such as Bill Maher, Roseanne Barr, Harry Shearer, Robert Klein, Al Franken, Steve Martin, Paul Reiser, Lizz Winstead, Richard Belzer, and Margaret Cho have all blogged on HuffPost. And top-shelf comedy writers, like Chris Kelly, Tony Hendra, Paul Krassner, and Adam McKay have demonstrated the power of good satire to simultaneously draw blood and evoke belly laughs.

Sometimes the joke was on us. Greg Gutfeld, then the editor of British *Maxim,* came to us via a recommendation. "Right off the bat, Greg started posting very strange, very off-the-wall stuff," Roy recalls. Because Gutfeld lived in London, these posts would often arrive in the middle of the night, leading the editors to wonder when they'd wake to more of his near Dadaist musings. Sometimes his satire took on HuffPost; he once claimed we were cosponsoring the first gay rights march to Mecca. "Some of our readers didn't know what to make of him," Roy says. "Some called for us to ban him. One or two other bloggers wondered about his sanity. But we loved the subversive, off-the-reservation vibe he brought to the site," which included "GREG'S DOUBLE SECRET HIDDEN BLOG!!! WELCOME TO MY TINY HOLE IN HELL!" "Unbeknownst to us, Gutfeld had turned his bio entry—which everyone else used to, well, list their bio—into a secret hidden blog where he railed endlessly about everything and anything," Roy says. "None of us noticed for weeks as he kept updating it with all manner of wild postings. When we finally stumbled upon this secret blog, hidden within our own site, we

HuffPost Humor

Larry David on Hillary Clinton's "red phone" ad during the 2008 Democratic primary:

I watched, transfixed, as she took the 3 A.M. call . . . and I was afraid . . . very afraid. Suddenly, I realized the last thing this country needs is that woman anywhere near a phone. I don't care if it's 3 A.M. or 10 P.M. or any other time. I don't want her talking to Putin, I don't want her talking to Kim Jong II, I don't want her talking to my nephew. She needs a long rest. She needs to put on a sarong and some sunblock and get away from things for a while, a nice beach somewhere—somewhere far away, where there are . . . no phones.

Al Franken on Mel Gibson's fall from grace:

So, I don't think Mel Gibson should be totally drummed out of the business. I think he should just have to start all over again. Put him in a movie as an "under-five" (an actor who has fewer than five lines). Make him play BUSBOY #2 in a Matthew McConaughey comedy.

Watching the dailies, a producer might say, "Hey, that busboy who said, 'You dropped your napkin, sir'—he's pretty good."

Then the director will say, "Of course he's good. That's Mel Gibson."

Bill Maher on Republican sex scandals:

Republicans changed their party before—from the party that freed the slaves to the party that freed Scooter Libby—and they survived. Now it's time for them to stop pretending they're still the party of Reagan and take up a new banner: the Party of Superfreaky Superfreaks.

This week, the chairman of the St. Petersburg, Florida, city council was accused of having sex with his two adopted daughters and their nanny. And he could have been in real trouble, too, if it turned out the nanny was an illegal. But he got ahead of the story when he killed himself by sitting in the garage with the doors closed and the riding lawn mower on.

Two guesses which party he was a member of. And the first guess doesn't count.

And that's not fair. You knew he was a Republican, because even in death, he was still wasting gas.

Republican sex scandals are getting to be like Iraqi car bombings. By the time you hear about one, there's been another. Ted Haggard, Mark Foley, Bob Allen, Vitter, Craig . . . It's like Clue, only the answer is always "A Republican . . . in the washroom . . . with his cock."

Steve Martin on Cheney gone mad:

Vice President Dick Cheney, while hunting wild geese in the Rose Garden, accidentally shot President Bush twice, once in the heart and once in the head. "I didn't really shoot the president twice," said Cheney. "The second time I shot him, I was president. It wasn't until my third shot, where I accidentally shot my own foot, that I had shot the president twice. I was officially injured and unable to govern, when Dennis Hastert came in, and stepped on the butt handle of the rifle causing it to swing up like a rake and shoot his hair off. I guess I'm officially responsible for that too, meaning I shot the acting president for a total of three occupants of the oval office. I'm not proud, but it is a record."

Nora Ephron on twenty-five things people have a shocking capacity to be surprised by over and over again:

1. Journalists sometimes make things up.
2. Journalists sometimes get things wrong.
3. Almost all books that are published as memoirs are initially written as novels, and then the agent/editor says, this might work better as a memoir.
4. Beautiful young women sometimes marry ugly, old rich men.
5. In business, there is no such thing as synergy in the good sense of the term.
6. Freedom of the press belongs to the man who owns one.
7. Nothing written in today's sports pages makes sense to anyone who didn't read yesterday's sports pages.
8. There is no explaining the stock market but people try.
9. The Democrats are deeply disappointing.
10. Movies have no political effect whatsoever.

11. High-protein diets work.

12. A lot of people take the Bible literally.

13. Pornography is the opiate of the masses.

14. You can never know the truth of anyone's marriage, including your own.

15. People actually sign pre-nuptial agreements.

16. Mary Matalin and James Carville are married.

17. Muslims hate us.

18. Everybody lies.

19. The reason why it's important for a Democrat to be president is the Supreme Court.

20. Howard Stern is apparently very nice in person.

21. In Manhattan a small one-bedroom apartment that needs work costs $1 million.

22. People look like their dogs.

23. Cary Grant was Jewish.

24. Cary Grant wasn't Jewish.

25. Larry King has never read a book.

Robert Klein on Larry Craig for vice president:

Rumors are flying out of the John McCain camp that a surprising and seemingly counterintuitive choice for the vice presidential running mate is imminent. There may be a proposal afoot among Republicans to name Senator Larry Craig of Idaho McCain's running mate. The theory being that if, as expected in November, after eight years of Bush incompetence the party's chances go into the toilet, Senator Craig is, among his party, the most well acquainted with the territory.

Lizz Winstead on the Bush administration's abstinence program:

You can preach and lecture and throw money at this issue until you are blue in the balls, and the result is going to be the same.

Teens are gonna have sex for three simple reasons:

1. It's fun
2. It's free
3. It's against your wishes

Wake up! When the most fun a person can ever have in the whole world is free, you can't stop it. Not even with twisting scientific facts like a balloon animal.

No, the only science that may work to prevent kids from having sex may be reverse psychology. Maybe if you sit your kids down and say, "When I grab your mother's firm buttocks and mount her like a stallion, she screams for the whip and God do I make her beg for it!"

After they've stopped throwing up, maybe they'll vow never to have sex.

We'll see how that turns out.

Adam McKay on the Bush administration's lack of foresight:

Two days before Katrina hit ground, me and some friends were talking at work about how vulnerable New Orleans is and how this hurricane could really devastate the city. Somehow we, a bunch of Hollywood flunkies on the set of a silly comedy, knew this and the Bush administration did not.

It was the same with bin Laden. After the bombing of the U.S.S. *Cole* I remember sitting with friends in a New York bar talking about the rise of the extremist threat in the Middle East and wondering if they would attack us here. And, keep in mind, Bush went to Yale and I went to Temple University. I still watch *SpongeBob* with my five-year-old daughter and laugh heartily at it. Dick Cheney does not watch *SpongeBob*. Though Condi did watch *Spamalot*.

So what were they doing that a bunch of dudes on a movie set knew this was coming and they did not? Obviously we're not that smart and the truth is half the country was having the same conversation. So what the frig? It's a really, really important question. Yet once again forty percent of the country calls these queries disgusting or unpatriotic. Maybe the sound of the word "query" makes them feel sexually uncomfortable.

were shocked—and delighted." His HuffPost blogs caught the attention of Fox News, and the network eventually gave him his own show, *Red Eye*.

Much of the credit for HuffPost's eclectic mix of bloggers goes to Arianna. Her constant refrain at dinner parties was, "That would be a great post!" or "You should write a blog for us." And many did. In an early e-mail to our bloggers, we offered them these pointers given to us by longtime blogger Mickey Kaus:

"Blogging is like good conversation. Make your point the way you would in an argument if you were trying to convince a friend. Make your point once and stop. Write about what interests you, not what you think you 'should' be writing about. Your first thought on how to put something is usually the best one—don't kill it with improvements. Takes that are quirky or eccentric or not the usual party line are a good thing."

Many of our bloggers are used to writing books, plays, or five-thousand-word glossy magazine features, so "Can you make it a little bloggier?" was a common editorial note. Roy recalls playwright Christopher Durang sending in a casual e-mail with four ideas for posts and his short take on each. "This e-mail is exactly the tone we want," Roy told him. "Smart, funny, personal, chatty. I could publish it as is."

Over time, these informal but informed posts from fascinating people have hooked millions of readers. With that kind of growing readership, we've been able to achieve one of our key goals: to have HuffPost become a contributor to the national conversation.

In terms of blogging and The Huffington Post itself, what I find so exciting—and relieving—is you can be watching the television and see something that upsets you, and you can walk to your computer, dash off an angry or concerned response to what you've just seen, and you can post it instantly, and suddenly it's out there.

It's online as quickly as it takes to send an e-mail. And there are no publishers and editors you have to pitch to or negotiate with—it's just out there.

—CHRISTOPHER DURANG, PLAYWRIGHT AND HUFFPOST BLOGGER

Not Politics as Usual

HuffPost's celebrity bloggers brought press attention, but it was our coverage of the Judith Miller controversy that really propelled us onto the national radar screen.

Judith Miller began her career in the Washington Bureau of *The New York Times* in 1977 and was named the Cairo Bureau chief in 1983. Due to the sources and friendships she developed there, she continued to cover the Middle East for years, even after returning to the U.S. In the run-up to the U.S.-led invasion of Iraq in 2003, she wrote numerous front-page *New York Times* articles about Saddam Hussein's pursuit of weapons of mass destruction. Bush administration officials pointed to her articles as supposedly "independent validation" of their case for the war. In May 2004, *The New York Times* admitted that it had relied heavily on discredited sources and other questionable information in several of its pre-Iraq-invasion articles. Miller's byline appeared on most of these pieces.

In the meantime, however, Miller had become involved in a legal matter that made the situation even more complicated than this extraordinary editorial mea culpa suggested. In early July 2003, Ambassador Joseph Wilson had written a *New York Times* editorial questioning some of the intelligence leading to the Iraq war. Shortly thereafter, Robert Novak revealed in a column that Wilson's wife, Valerie Plame, was a covert CIA agent. It turned out that Miller and *Time* reporter Matthew Cooper had also somehow learned this information, potentially through conversations with administration officials. Miller was subpoenaed to testify to a federal grand jury about the leak, but she refused on the grounds that journalists have a right to protect their sources. She was subsequently jailed for eighty-five days, starting July 7, 2005.

Eventually Scooter Libby, Cheney's former chief of staff, gave her permission to testify, and she was released. Some saw Miller as a First Amendment hero.

HuffPost had a very different take. On July 27, 2005, less than three weeks after Miller started serving time in the Alexandria City Jail, Arianna blogged that Miller "certainly wasn't an innocent writer caught up in the whirl of history. She had a starring role in it . . . Re-reading some of her pre-war reporting today, it's hard not to be disgusted by how inaccurate and pumped up it turned out to be." Rather than a First Amendment martyr, Miller was little more than a White House shill.

Over the course of many months, Arianna regularly blogged about the Miller story, dissecting each new piece of information as it came out. Mainstream media sources began picking up these takes, and writers around the blogosphere regularly linked to them. In the end, even *The New York Times'* own narrative about Miller started to shift. She resigned from her job at the paper in November 2005.

Beyond the Miller controversy, our coverage of the Valerie Plame affair produced a few other special HuffPost moments:

JUDY, JUDY, JUDY
ROY SEKOFF, EDITOR, THE HUFFINGTON POST

The Judy Miller story was a turning point for HuffPost—both in our own realization of the impact we could have on a story and in how it changed the way others perceived us. People saw us being out front in reshaping opinion on an important story. And when others turned to our way of thinking, it increased our credibility and cast us in a different light.

The major thrust of Arianna's reporting/blogging on the Miller story was the way it relentlessly and assiduously, point by point and piece by piece, kept the spotlight on *The New York Times'* handling of Miller—examining and deconstructing *Times* editorials, memos, meetings, and behind-the-scenes maneuverings—and, in the process, revealed a very dysfunctional journalistic culture (self-protective and self-denying), a culture that isn't unique to the *Times*.

By using the paper's own words and actions to build a case—and keeping up the drumbeat and the questioning in a very public forum that was increasingly drawing the attention of other media sources—Arianna and HuffPost turned largely behind-the-scenes players like editor Bill Keller and publisher Arthur Sulzberger into lead actors in a tragicomic production of their own making. What's more, HuffPost became a place for frustrated staffers inside the *Times* to give information. Insiders began to see that this was a place where they could get their opinions aired—and that it would have a real impact.

From the beginning, Arianna's blog posts succeeded in blowing holes in Miller's reporting by collecting all the damning facts already known about Miller in one place. Taken in their entirety, and put into a frame that presented Miller not as a First Amendment martyr but as someone complicit in the Bush administration's attempts to sell the war in Iraq to the American people, these facts spoke for themselves and laid waste to Miller's noble-reporter-going-to-jail-to-preserve-the-integrity-of-journalism image.

In more than forty posts written over the course of thirteen months, Arianna eviscerated Judy Miller's claims—whether delivered from the courthouse, the jailhouse, in her post-release TV appearances, or in her self-serving explanation in the *Times*.

It's very hard to spin the truth when you have someone checking everything you say and write.

- Within minutes of President Bush commuting Scooter Libby's sentence (for his role in identifying Plame), we had a blog lineup filled with immediate reaction and analysis, including posts from Paul Begala, Jane Smiley, Marty Kaplan, and Matt Cooper, the *Time* reporter whose conversations with Libby led, in part, to Libby's indictment.

- One of the jurors in the Scooter Libby trial, reporter Denis Collins, chose to tell his story through HuffPost. We were able to give him all the real estate he wanted. No traditional print publication could.

The 2008 Election: Getting OffTheBus

One of the most innovative HuffPost projects has been our OffTheBus coverage of the 2008 presidential campaign. This joint venture between HuffPost and New York University journalism professor Jay Rosen provides a platform for nearly eight thousand citizen journalists to report on the men and women vying to be president and has become "a force in journalism, even as it challenges the standard notions of traditional journalism," Katherine Q. Seelye wrote in *The New York Times.* It has also produced some of the campaign season's biggest scoops.

Here is a bit of background on the project: Any political junkie knows that modern presidential campaigns work long hours to shape the public's perception of their candidate. In a country of three hundred million people, most citizens will never meet their president, nor anyone who aspires to the office. What they can do is visit a candidate's website or watch their speeches on YouTube—and a growing number of Americans do that—but much of peoples' relationship with the candidate is established by the work of journalists in mainstream television, radio, and print.

So it behooves any smart presidential aspirant to surround himself (or herself) with people who know how to work the media. Specifically, these handlers need to work the beat journalists who follow the candidate around on their bus or plane—a reality of coverage since journalist Timothy Crouse's book, *The Boys on the Bus*, recounted the 1972 contest between President Richard Nixon and Senator George McGovern. Campaigns build a rapport with the journalists who must spend weeks or even months listening to the same speeches over and over again. They reward journalists who write positive coverage.

What has worked well for campaigns doesn't necessarily best serve the public. And that's why Arianna Huffington and Jay Rosen, a pioneer in the concept of "civic journalism," founded OffTheBus.

With the rise of Internet tools that made interactivity more possible, Rosen had started Newassignment.net, an experiment in "open source" reporting, in July 2006. The purpose of this experiment was to allow large numbers of professional and amateur journalists to work together on projects. Since a big part of HuffPost's appeal is how it mixes reporting and opinion from people of all walks of life, Arianna knew a good fit when she saw one. The two organizations teamed up to tap the power of citizen journalists to cover the presidential campaign in July 2007. They hired Amanda Michel, a former Dean and Kerry online political organizer, to direct the project, and Marc Cooper, an award-winning veteran journalist, as its editor.

At the time of its launch more than three hundred of HuffPost's readers and bloggers signed up for the project. One year later, more than eight thousand people had joined OffTheBus.

OffTheBus is an attempt to forge a new model of journalism in the crucible of an election season. The evolution of digital technologies has opened the door to a democratization of journalism. OffTheBus has tried to kick it open. The project has empowered

Our idea is not complicated: It's campaign reporting by a great many more people than would ever fit on the bus that the boys (and girls) of the press have famously gotten on and off every four years, as they try to cover the race for president.

—JAY ROSEN

ON BLOGGERS AND IDEAS
THAT CHANGE EVERYTHING

CRAIG NEWMARK, FOUNDER OF CRAIGSLIST.ORG AND HUFFPOST BLOGGER

Victor Hugo spoke of an "idea whose time is come." Bloggers are the spokesmen of such ideas, like Martin Luther and the Reformation, or John Locke and Thomas Paine regarding representative democracy. Now we have many bloggers advocating participatory democracy, and that changes all of American politics.

thousands of non-card-carrying journalists to go out and commit random and not-so-random acts of journalism. In exchange, OffTheBus offers its members editorial support and guidance.

There aren't many seats on the bus or the plane, and let's face it, the $2,000-per-day campaign plane ticket isn't one that most journalists, or citizens, can afford. Instead of relying on the insider stream of information produced from within a tightly managed bubble, OffTheBus members have unwittingly broken down the walls between the campaign and the public, and ushered in an engaged citizenry ready to report on those who want to govern in its name.

When traditional reporting tactics don't work, OffTheBus uses a collaborative methodology it developed for producing unique stories beyond the scope of a single reporter. Back in October 2007 OffTheBus used this technique to report first on the significance of the economy as a voting issue. Over and over again its members have fanned out, conducting hundreds of interviews with evangelical ministers, GOP county chairs, and elected officials to report on trends happening around the country.

OffTheBus members are moms and dads, grandmas and

COMMITTING ACTS OF JOURNALISM

Q&A WITH DAVID WEINER, HUFFPOST BLOGGER

David Weiner scored a scoop with his revelation that John McCain's wife, Cindy, had lifted several "McCain Family Recipes"—which the McCain camp included on the campaign website—directly from the Food Network website. She'd also given *Family Circle* her favorite cookie recipe—lifted almost verbatim from Hersheys.com. He tells his story below.

HUFFPOST: How did you get the scoop for the first story about Cindy McCain's recipes? How did breaking the first story lead to breaking the second?

WEINER: The first scoop came through my dad, of all people. A woman he works with named Lauren Handel had mentioned in passing that she had discovered the recipe fraud by accident while searching for recipes on the Internet. Aware of my connection with The Huffington Post, my dad and Lauren called me to see if I was interested in writing something about it. And honestly, at first I wasn't. I didn't think anyone was going to care, and I wasn't crazy about putting out a story that seemed to be based purely on frivolous details. Like many people, I'm not crazy about the direction of political reporting, and a story like this seemed to me to just be adding to the pile. But after sitting down to write up the post, I realized that there was more to the story than first met the eye and that maybe this could open up certain avenues of discussion that had been more or less closed before, from Cindy McCain's greatly ignored drug problems and subsequent theft of pills from her charity, to the absurdity of the fact that our first wives (or husbands) are still required to pretend they're Suzy Homemaker when in fact they are often so much more.

The second story came from a completely random source. I guess someone had the insight or sense to check on other recipes put out by the McCain campaign, and lo and behold they had used the same old playbook and run a plagiarized recipe. I suppose my name and The Huffington Post became associated with the original Recipe-gate story, so the tipster brought it to us. That's the nice thing about the Internet and blogging that's also very different from print or television journalism: Readers feel like you're much more accessible or closer to them, and therefore they are more apt to send you tips or links or really just keep an eye out for things that may relate to whatever you've written. It's incredibly easy to track somebody down on the Internet, especially when they have their own blog. It's significantly more difficult to get in contact with a newspaperman or TV pundit—I know, I've tried.

HUFFPOST: What was the reaction to the story like? What surprised you about the attention it got?

WEINER: The response to the story was crazy. Really, I didn't see half that stuff coming. I remember lying in bed the night before the story broke, thinking to myself that it would probably get picked up by some of the more liberal blogs and maybe get some blips in the mainstream media. But I knew, *knew* that the McCain campaign was going to have to issue some statement about it, whatever it may be, and that blew me away. I was (and still am) a nobody, just a guy with the right information and the right outlet, and one of two finalists in the most important contest in the world was going to have to apologize because of something I did.

But things got crazier. The story was picked up by every major news media organization in the country and many around the world. The blogs were going wild about it and people I hadn't spoken to in years were contacting me to see if it was the same David Weiner they knew. I was even asked to do a radio interview about it, which made my day. Yet all this was going on while I was at the office for my day job, so I had to keep it on the down low. I scheduled the conference room so I could do my interview in private and kept my head down the whole day. I didn't even tell anyone in my office about it until the next day when my name was in *The Washington Post* and *The New York Times*.

> **HUFFPOST**: What did you learn from doing these posts and from the reaction they got?
>
> **WEINER**: First, I learned that it's not a good idea to become a public figure when your last name is "Weiner" (Lawrence Weiner and Congressman Anthony Weiner aside). This is especially true if your claim to fame is food related. And it's even more true when Fox News hires people like Greg Gutfeld to sling first-grade-level insults at you while smirking at the camera for five minutes straight (though I'll admit, despite missing the whole point of the story, he had a couple of funny lines).

grandpas, doctors, lawyers, educators, waitresses, retired journalists, and schoolkids. Ethan Hova, the OffTheBus member who broke the news that presidential contender Mitt Romney paid Christian activists to write favorable coverage of his campaign, is a Shakespearean actor. Chicago-based writer Christine Escobar joined OffTheBus and since then has launched several citizen journalism sites. R. T. Eby files dispatches from Appalachia, where he tends okra fields. Who knows, maybe your neighbor participates in HuffPost's OffTheBus.

HuffPost Bloggers and the '08 Race

Through OffTheBus and its regular political coverage, HuffPost broke a number of stories through the 2007 run-up to the primaries and the primaries themselves. Our best-known scoop, however, hit the page in April 2008 and has since become known as "Bittergate."

In July 2007, sixty-year-old Mayhill Fowler began to blog for us as part of the OffTheBus project. She describes herself in her HuffPost bio as an "overeducated" woman "with politics in my blood." She followed the Obama campaign to several locations at her own expense. In keeping with HuffPost policies, she disclosed her support for Obama's candidacy and the fact that she donated to his campaign. On April 6, during the run-up to the contentious Pennsylvania primary, she found herself at a private Obama fund-raiser in San Francisco. In general, high-end fund-raising events are closed to the press, but at the time of this event there were no stated rules barring bloggers. Fowler arrived with tape recorder in hand. No one asked her to turn it off. So Fowler recorded Obama's talk. He said a number of things, but this quote struck her as news:

> You go into some of these small towns in Pennsylvania, and like a lot of small towns in the Midwest, the jobs have been gone now for twenty-five years and nothing's replaced them. And they fell through the Clinton administration, and the Bush administration, and each successive administration has said that somehow these communities are gonna regenerate and they have not. And it's not surprising then they get bitter, they cling to guns or religion or antipathy to people who aren't like them or anti-immigrant sentiment or anti-trade sentiment as a way to explain their frustrations.

She was right. When she uploaded the audio file to HuffPost a few days later, the post got five thousand comments within forty-eight hours. It was picked up by the Associated Press and every other major media outlet. Fowler herself became the subject of much press attention, particularly when she scored another scoop. In early June, at an event in South Dakota, Fowler asked former president Bill Clinton if a *Vanity Fair* profile of him was weighing on his mind. He unleashed a stream of insults against writer Todd Purdham. The resulting audio clip helped build the story that the former president might be losing his political golden touch as his wife's presidential chances sank.

Bittergate demonstrated to anyone who was paying attention that modern campaigns must be aware of what some call their Digital Miranda Rights—i.e., everything you say in any venue can and will be used against you. The Obama campaign, a few days after this bitter quote went 'round the world, publicly made this concession. Campaign spokesperson Bill Burton told the *San Francisco Chronicle* that, indeed, the fund-raiser that Folwer attended "was closed to the press but not off the record." Fowler's story not only had a dramatic impact on the campaign, it also reshaped the protocols of contemporary political reporting. The old media met the new.

In our world of camera phones and the like, there are no real "off the record" moments anymore. And in our wired, interactive media universe, we can all report news as it happens. So the distinction between press and public has blurred to the point of being irrelevant. We tend to think that's a good thing—a service that the OffTheBus project is providing. Why shouldn't people know what the candidates vying to lead them think—particularly in the unguarded moments not available to the boys on the bus?

HuffPost—It's Not Just About Politics . . .

From the beginning, HuffPost has always featured stories on a wide range of topics: politics, media, entertainment, sex, religion, relationships, you name it. Indeed, one of our early opinion-

SPOTLIGHT ON MAYHILL FOWLER

CITIZEN JOURNALIST AND HUFFPOST BLOGGER

HUFFPOST: What have you learned about blogging?

FOWLER: Truth will win out. This is the most important thing that should shape anybody's reporting. This is why, at least in my opinion, partisan political blogging is of short-term value only. No matter how much a partisan political blogger tries to nudge his or her candidate forward, the effort is wasted if it isn't in the service of finding the real story. The value of partisan blogs lies elsewhere—in the community of like-minded bloggers and commenters, in the feelings of belonging and mattering and validation that membership provides. This is a worthwhile pursuit, but it's not reporting.

HUFFPOST: What advice would you give to new bloggers?

FOWLER: The best [general] advice I can give on the subject of trying to find the truth of the matter is to do a self-check regularly: "I know what I'm looking at, but what am I really seeing?"

And here is my specific advice:

Not just Google. Googling is a great help but is not the final word in research. You'd be surprised how many reporters writing about me relied upon Google gossip and therefore said (making themselves ridiculous in the eyes of everyone I know) that 1) my husband is a McCain contributor (he is in fact a lifelong Democrat who volunteered for the McGovern campaign); 2) my husband (or my husband and I) own a yacht or yachts in Turkey.

Get the details. Here is [OffTheBus editor] Marc Cooper's advice to me from last summer, and I've found it to be the absolute best. "You're creating a body of work," he said, "and you're laying down the historical record."

Forget luck. It's all about hard work. Those two scoops on Obama and Clinton for which I'm known didn't just happen. I got the Obama story because I'd been following his campaign in California from June 2007, at a time when other journalists weren't all that interested, and had made contacts within the campaign. And when Obama spoke at the San Francisco fund-raiser, like him I had just come from Pennsylvania, where I had been observing and writing about his campaign, and therefore I, unlike the other people present, knew exactly what he had never said before. As for Bill Clinton, I saw him at twenty-four of his more than three hundred small-town campaign stops before the one in South Dakota that was big news [because of his statements about Todd Purdham]. I knew the Bill Clinton of 2008 very well by that time.

Write, write, write. I wrote five hours a day for fifteen years before [OffTheBus project director] Amanda Michel gave me a platform for my writing at OffTheBus. During those fifteen years, I thought I was writing stories and novels, but what I was really doing was honing the art and craft of writing. Emphasis on *craft*—which brings me back to reading. A. J. Liebling. E. B. White. John Hersey, Hunter Thompson, Mark Twain. Study the masters as you develop your own style.

shaping moments came courtesy of a story that ran in the entertainment pages of many other publications.

Early in the morning on July 26, 2006, director Mel Gibson was pulled over on a California highway and arrested for driving under the influence. Rather than apologizing to the officers for his behavior, he chose that moment to launch into an anti-Semitic spiel about how Jews had caused all the world's wars. The entertainment blog TMZ broke the story of his arrest on the evening of July 28. The next day, Gibson issued an apology for his drinking but did not directly acknowledge his anti-Semitism. Everyone in Hollywood seemed to be waiting—looking to see if other people would condemn this powerful director's statements or just brush them under the rug as the rantings of a confused drunk.

Then, on July 30, agent Ari Emanuel brought the conversation into the open in a blog on HuffPost: "I wish Mel Gibson well in dealing with his alcoholism, but alcoholism does not excuse racism and anti-Semitism," he wrote. "It is one thing when marginal figures with no credibility make anti-Semitic statements. It is a completely different thing when a figure of Mel Gibson's stature does so." Emanuel concluded his post with a call for others to confront Gibson's behavior directly: "People in the entertainment community, whether Jew or gentile, need to demonstrate that they understand how much is at stake in this by professionally shunning Mel Gibson and refusing to work with him, even if it means a sacrifice to their bottom line."

The next day, Arianna wrote a post on Gibson's arrest that praised Emanuel's initiative and seconded his call for others to take a public stand against the actor. "I see the Gibson story as 'a moment of opportunity,' a chance for reasonable people to stand up and be counted," she wrote. "But is Ari the only high-profile figure willing to publicly draw a line in the Malibu sand? How disgusting and disappointing is that?" Then the silence began to lift, and figures such as Barbara Walters declared, "I'll never go see a Mel Gibson movie again." In short order, more influential people in Hollywood stepped forward and called Gibson to account, including Sony Pictures chairwoman Amy Pascal, producers Arnon Milchan and Laura Ziskin, and manager Bernie Brillstein—earning themselves, in Arianna's words "a plaque in the Backbone Hall of Fame."

Gibson eventually offered a more specific and heartfelt apology. And the power of a well-timed blog was reconfirmed. As Arianna wrote: "By taking an immediate and unambiguous stand on Sunday, Ari Emanuel showed that not everyone in town was willing to write off Gibson's odious racism as the cost of doing business with a bankable hit maker."

We've had coverage like this from the beginning. But as the amount of content submitted to HuffPost continued to grow, we knew we needed to expand our ability to feature all of it. So in May 2007 we created what we call "verticals." These subject areas—Politics, Business, Living, Media, Entertainment, and our summer 2008 addition of Style and Green verticals—roughly mimic the sections in a newspaper. Like the original home page, they feature news aggregation on the right and blog posts on the left. Now, roughly half our traffic goes to these verticals.

They, too, have produced some memorable HuffPost moments:

- When *Sicko* director Michael Moore went on *Larry King Live* to debate Dr. Sanjay Gupta, who'd criticized various facts in Moore's film, he first posted on HuffPost documentation to back up his claim that CNN had knowingly aired inaccurate information and directed Larry King viewers to check out the paperwork on our site. And, after his Larry King appearance, Moore logged on to HuffPost for a live chat, during which our users were able to ask him follow-up questions.

- Actor Rob Lowe used HuffPost to break news of an impending lawsuit against his family in April 2008: "A former employee is demanding my wife Sheryl and I pay her $1.5 million by the end of the week or she will accuse us both of a vicious laundry list of false terribles," he wrote. His post allowed him to get out in front of the media firestorm that was sure to result from the lawsuit and present his side of the story—unfiltered and very personal.

- Drawing on her own experiences with controversial photos, Jamie Lee Curtis blogged on HuffPost about Miley Cyrus's "topless" (or backless, as the case may be) photos in *Vanity Fair:* "I know how Miley feels. I too was a little embarrassed by my recent topless 'scandal' [on the cover of *AARP the Magazine*] and the subsequent parodies, but I am an adult woman. I protected myself during the shoot and I can take the heat. I only wish that her guardians had protected her."

We were also pleased to become a go-to site for the latest news and opinion on the writer's strike that divided Hollywood in the fall of 2007. HuffPost bloggers, many of them members of the striking guild, took to our blog to express their outrage and to try to make their case. Chris Kelly, a longtime writer for Bill Maher and one of HuffPost's most popular bloggers, used his post to explain to the layman, in his inimitable style, one of the key issues of the strike—residual payments: "A residual isn't a handout or an allowance or Paris Hilton's trust fund. It's not a lottery payout, or alimony, or an annuity from a slip and fall accident at a casino. A residual is a deferred payment against the lifetime value of a script. It's not a perk. It's okay if you didn't know that. It's in the best interests of a lot of fairly large corporations that you don't. And it makes it easier to imagine that writers are asking for something workers don't deserve."

We published over 250 blog posts on the strike; taken as a whole they offer a very personal snapshot of Hollywood at the time.

As you can see, there are no limits to the subjects you can blog about. Arianna's output since we launched (over 1,200 posts—and counting) is proof that anything is fair game. Although she has built a reputation as one of the country's top political commentators, she has also written about a host of nonpolitical topics, ranging from the offbeat to the highly personal. Here's a small sampling:

On her devastation at dropping her BlackBerry in the Mediterranean: "From the moment we were introduced, we became close. Inseparable. Too close, some suggested. Friends began to whisper that the relationship was taking up more and more of my time, energy, and focus. But I didn't realize how intense things had gotten until my constant companion was lost at sea and the grief set in. Yes, it's true. I'm one of the more than three million Americans who have been utterly seduced by the charms of the little Canadian wireless device."

On the negative effects of sleep deprivation: "Getting enough sleep signifies to some people that you must be less than passionate about your work and your life. It means, well, you're lazy. Very often women workaholics forego sleep, because they've bought into the mentality that says sleep time is unproductive time. Yet what have all this workaholism and sleep loss bought us? Less productivity, less job satisfaction, less sex, and more inches around the waist. Doesn't seem like a very good deal, does it? So do yourself a favor and go to sleep right after sex. Or before sex. Or instead of sex. Just not during sex."

On orgasms: "Wouldn't it be delicious if the female orgasm were the thing that tips the scales in favor of the Intelligent Design crowd? It would make for a great closing argument: 'The female orgasm is so complex and strange, it could only have come from God. The reason there is no evolutionary purpose to it is because there is no evolution! God is in the details . . . and the bedroom. Who needs Darwin when you have the Bible—and the Jack Rabbit vibrator. Case closed. Amen.' "

On counterfeit Italian cheese: "According to Agenzia Nazionale Stampa Associata, an Italian news agency, nine out of ten Italian cheeses sold in America are fakes—that is, not really made in Italy . . . But it's not just Parmigiano Reggiano that is being counterfeited faster than the latest Kate Spade bag. If you're partial to Fontina, there's a good chance that it's coming from China, and if you're enjoying what you think is Asiago, instead of coming from Northern Italy, it's probably from Wisconsin."

On the media's overuse of the dreaded "ham sandwich" analogy: "It was inevitable. As soon as the DeLay indictment was announced, you just knew that shopworn references to a grand jury indicting a certain lunchtime favorite wouldn't be far behind. And, indeed, the ham sandwich analogies were flying last night on the cable shows. 'Everybody says you can indict a ham sandwich with a grand jury,' said the man of the hour himself, Tom DeLay, on *Hardball.* 'This is a ham sandwich indictment without the ham.' Picking up this latest GOP talking-point twist on the cliché was Rep. Ileana Ros-Lehtinen, who told Larry King: 'This is a ham sandwich indictment with one correction. There's no ham in the sandwich.' Over on Fox, Charles Krauthammer piled on, adding his own 'special sauce' to the mix: 'As the lawyers like to say, you can indict a ham sandwich and . . . Tom DeLay is going to be a Big Mac for [the prosecutor].' Putting aside the question of DeLay's similarity to a ham sandwich, and the ease with which a prosecutor could indict either of them, can we all agree that the time has come to retire the metaphor? I mean, there are lots of other perfectly good sandwiches on the menu. Why not 'You can indict a hot pastrami sandwich'? Or a roast beef sandwich? Or turkey and swiss? Or tongue? Or any of the salads (tuna, chicken or egg)? Or, for health conscious indictees, avocado and sprouts on pita? In any case, the Deli Defense definitely needs some fresh meat."

On the connection between oral sex, bike seats, and the trials and tribulations of being the mother of teenage daughters: "I'm sitting here at LAX about to board a flight to Boston to bring my sixteen-year-old daughter home from school for Christmas. Next to me is a bagful of reading I've been meaning to catch up on, including yet another study showing that young women are 'tearing down sexual taboos,' 'are far less prudish,' and are 'having sex at a younger age.'

"Help me out, readers: What's a (theoretically) enlightened mother of two teenage daughters to make of this information? On the one hand, it's clearly a good thing that, over the course of the five decades the study spanned, 'feelings of sexual guilt plummeted, especially among young women.' I'm certainly all for guilt-free sex—but not for kids. Especially mine! I mean, young girls are now, on average, starting to have intercourse at fifteen. Fifteen! The study also shows a skyrocketing increase in oral sex. According to the co-author of the report: 'Oral sex has become so popular. In previous generations, oral sex was considered disgusting. Now young people see it as another way of being sexual.' I get it: 'friends with benefits.' Oh. My. God.

"Reading this report, my first instinct was to go online and Google 'chastity belts.' Luckily, my catch-up reading bag also included a *New York Times* article showing that bike seats can seriously affect sexual prowess. According to a urologist who has studied the problem: 'There are only two kinds of male cyclists—those who are impotent and those who will be impotent.' It was a eureka moment: So, from now on, my teenage daughters will not be allowed to date a boy who doesn't put in at least seventy-five miles a week on his ten-speed."

On Ann Coulter: "Coulter is the right wing punditry's equivalent of crack or crystal meth. She's highly addictive—giving users the delirious, giddy high of outrageousness. But then the buzz wears off and they come crashing down, their spirits shriveled, their souls poisoned. Her brand of way, way over-the-top rhetoric, trading on hatred, demonizing, and caricature, is doing to the American body politic what a three-month meth bender does to crank junkies."

On Stephen Colbert's instant-classic scorched-earth performance at the 2006 White House Correspondents' Dinner: "It was a quintessential 'All About Eve'—I mean, 'All About Steve'—moment: He walked up to that podium a basic-cable cult figure, and came back a political comedy legend. Start carving that satiric Mt. Rushmore: Swift, Twain, Bruce . . . Colbert."

On visiting Gore Vidal in Italy, which offered an occasion to reflect on the Iraq war: "Sitting on Gore's terrace, overlooking one of the most breathtaking spots on earth—what Gore called the heart of Magna Graecia, the part of southern Italy that was colonized by Greeks and later conquered by Romans—it felt like we were on top of history. A history of dreams of empire, and of lessons unlearned. Gore, such a brilliant chronicler of so much of this history, reminded us how foreign to our national character the neocons' imperial dreams are. 'Americans have always favored minding our own business,' he told us. 'From George Washington to John Quincy Adams, the American way has been to avoid imperial adventures.' He then cited Adams' famous admonition that America 'goes not abroad in search of monsters to destroy. She is the well-wisher to the freedom and independence of all. She is the champion and vindicator only of her own.' So it's part of our national DNA to shun Iraqs—and to want to get out of them."

On the passing of her father-in-law, Roy Huffington, whose name The Huffington Post bears: "When our girls were little, I remember he used to patiently take them outside and teach them about the plants and the soil. He did this with such passion and depth of knowledge that, at one point or another, each of his granddaughters expressed a desire to follow in his footsteps as a geologist. They all eventually broke off from the geology track, but stayed close to him."

Up to the Moment

The Huffington Post began its life in Arianna's living room. These days, we operate out of three offices—in New York, Los Angeles, and Washington, DC. The majority of our news and blog teams are located in the SoHo neighborhood of New York. Our politics coverage is spearheaded by a team of five editors and reporters working out of an office on K Street in Washington, DC. About six people work out of Arianna's house in Brentwood, California. Arianna, as editor in chief, and Roy, as the site's editor, work wherever they happen to be, which is often shuttling between all these offices, or at home. Someone is monitoring the news and dealing with new blog posts at all hours of the day. Sometimes it's easy to forget that only four years have passed since a disappointing election sparked the construction of the "pioneering bridge," as Gary Hart has so graciously dubbed us. Four hectic, challenging, exhilarating, and very satisfying years.

CHAPTER 7

HOW THE BLOGOSPHERE IS REMAKING THE MEDIA

Bloggers speak truth to power and are starting to fill the
checks and balances role formerly performed by the
conventional press. The best in blogging pursues the truth,
with fact-checking comparable to the best of the press.
—*Craig Newmark, founder of Craigslist.org and HuffPost blogger*

Confession: Many of us here at The Huffington Post are newspaper junkies.

We may be "new media," but curling up with the Sunday morning paper and a big mug of coffee is a highlight of our weekends. On weekdays, we like to smack a newspaper down on our desks and scan the headlines as a way to ease into work. There's something inherently satisfying about a neatly designed front page. The text looks authoritative. The pictures are gripping. Some of us have dreamed of seeing our bylines printed on the darn things since we read the newspaper as twelve-year-olds, sitting at the end of the driveway, waiting for the school bus.

But, young as many staffers are, that was still a few years ago. You can't drop by Jim Romenesko's Media News (one of the industry's first blogs) without noting all the industry's woes. In 2008, thousands of jobs at dozens of newspapers across the country—

including *The New York Times*, *Los Angeles Times*, *Chicago Tribune*, and *The Washington Post*—have been eliminated. A reader even sued the Raleigh, North Carolina, *News & Observer*, claiming that he wouldn't have renewed his subscription if he knew the paper planned to cut its staff and news pages as much as it has of late. Phil Meyer, a longtime professor at the University of North Carolina's school of journalism, claims that the last print edition of a newspaper will be published some morning in April 2043.

Well, that isn't exactly what he said (we're a blog—we checked). Newspaper publishers would have to be pretty stubborn to keep printing copies for that last lone reader. But in his 2004 book, *The Vanishing Newspaper: Saving Journalism in the Information Age*, Meyer does show a scatter plot of the declining percentage of Americans who read a daily newspaper. If you draw a line, it does zero out somewhere in a recycling bin around that fateful morning.

Contrary to the flushed belief in some parts of the blogosphere, blogs are not the main reason for this decline. It's a hard truth of the modern world that much of media is advertising dollars seeking eyeballs. Mass media—which includes most newspapers—tries to reach too many people with too varied interests for advertisers to target their dollars precisely. In the past, advertisers accepted this because there were no other options. But today, if you sell kitchen tile, why advertise on the evening news when you can advertise on a cable TV home renovation show for a fraction of the price? Or, even better, on a sidebar on Google when you know someone has specifically searched for kitchen tile? Craigslist—the online portal for jobs, stuff, love, etc.—has eaten up big chunks of the newspaper classifieds' market by charging nothing or next to it for a service newspapers have long considered a cash cow. In addition, younger people tend to like to customize their media consumption in a way that an evening news show or a daily print newspaper doesn't allow. For a variety of reasons (including more malleable buying habits), advertisers are more excited about reaching younger consumers than older consumers. As the mainstream media audience ages, advertising dollars drift away.

Mainstream media has been called "dinosaur media" by some on the web, but extinction is not imminent. Big-city daily newspapers and the network news still have millions of loyal readers and viewers—far more than most blogs. Plus, lots of bloggers comment on mainstream media stories. If the dinosaur media disappear like giant lizards after an asteroid strike, these bloggers could be bound for a similar fate.

But blogs are hastening changes in the media landscape with their informality, immediacy, and openness to all comers, and old-timers in musty newsrooms have been following suit. At other times, though, it seems that "newspaper editors really believe that everybody reads the paper the way they did, starting on page one and going all the way through," says Meyer. "The one-size-fits-all model doesn't work in the information age."

So the models are changing to adapt to new technology and new habits. What's emerging now is a fascinating hybrid of old-style news and blogging—it is what HuffPost aims to do. Plenty of other news outlets are finding it works as well.

"Newspapers to Bloggers: DROP DEAD"—Until They Didn't

"I used to subscribe to a print newspaper seven days a week," Jim Romenesko tells us. Now he gets *The New York Times* on weekends and the *Chicago Tribune* a few days a week. Obviously, a man who

HOW THE "FATHER OF THE UNDERGROUND PRESS" COMMUNICATES WITHOUT COMPROMISE

PAUL KRASSNER, AUTHOR OF *ONE HAND JERKING: REPORTS FROM AN INVESTIGATIVE SATIRIST* AND HUFFPOST BLOGGER

In 1958, I launched a magazine called *The Realist*. My mission was to communicate without compromise. My slogan was "Irreverence is our only sacred cow." I never labeled an article as either journalism or satire because I didn't want to deprive readers of the pleasure of discerning for themselves whether something was true or an extension of the truth. When *People* magazine labeled me "father of the underground press," I immediately demanded a paternity test.

In 2001, I decided to publish the final issue of *The Realist*. One reason was that home computers enabled *anyone* to communicate without compromise and with a minimum of expense. Now I can blog on the Internet whenever the urge strikes me. Although I still write for print magazines—with a lead time of four months—the web provides virtual immediacy to the process of spreading information, misinformation, disinformation, opinion, entertainment, insight, and triviality. I used to be a Luddite, but I'm becoming almost as much in awe of technology as I am of Nature.

professionally covers the newspaper industry still reads newspapers. But he can read them online. And what he's reading online looks a lot different than the static newspaper homepages of the late 1990s. "Newspapers are picking up on blogs, seeing it as a way to add value to the property," he says.

The New York Times, for instance, now has dozens of blogs, tracking everything from Iraq (Baghdad Bureau), to baseball (Bats), to technology (Bits), to climate change (Dot Earth). The *Los Angeles Times* has a blog (The Homicide Report) tracking every murder in the city. And as we were writing this, the *Daily Telegram* in Superior, Wisconsin, announced that it would focus far more of its limited resources on the web and scale back its print edition to twice a week. It's a far cry from the Web 1.0 days when the website of a newspaper was seen as a place for the cub reporters to amuse themselves.

Granted, news outlets were slow to jump on the blogging bandwagon. "I think a lot of times newspapers move somewhat slowly because of bureaucracies and traditions," Romenesko says. "I think originally there was a resistance to blogs—I think the mind-set was that blogs are the enemy. It took a while for higher levels of editors to accept that they're not the enemy, and why don't we become bloggers ourselves."

That was a smart move for these visionaries, because mainstream media outlets that start blogs realize quickly that they have natural advantages in the blogging game. "The newspaper blogs have, number one, resources, number two, contacts, and also readership," Romenesko says. Reporters have Rolodexes full of sources (or more likely, electronic address books full of contacts, but you know what we mean). When these professional reporters start blogging, they can call up their contacts to make or comment on the news. Amateur bloggers might have trouble getting people to return their calls. Furthermore, a *New York Times* blog has a built-in audience. An amateur blogger would have to build up to that level of readership and credibility. That doesn't mean she can't do it, but in a world of unlimited content, a big brand name helps a lot.

On a more fundamental level, every print and broadcast media outlet now updates its website regularly. This reality—and the plethora of mainstream media columns that are specifically labeled as blogs—changes the blogs and newspapers story from one of conflict to one of symbiosis. Like back-scratching apes, they help each other. The mainstream media breaks a lot of stories that bloggers run with. Bloggers break some stories that major media outlets then cover. "I think the whole debate is really silly and moot at this point," Romenesko says. "Newspapers accept blogging, and bloggers link to newspapers."

Indeed, one of the most fascinating developments in the blogosphere is the creation of new hybrid newspaper/blogs that have never existed in print form. With its various sections from Living to Business, HuffPost is probably the best-known hybrid, but there are others. The *MinnPost,* a web property which bills itself as "High-quality journalism for people who care about Minnesota," features frequent updates. There's even a *MinnPost in Print* edition which is actually a PDF you can print if the ink costs are worth it to you. Its business model is to solicit donations from people who want to see good local coverage. It's raked in over $1 million so far. The *Chi-Town Daily News* in Chicago is another online newspaper that publishes updates as its mostly volunteer writers send them in.

Plenty of us would mourn the total loss of a newspaper form that gets ink on our hands as we drink our coffee. But as more people have handheld devices for reading headlines during a commute, and as more people read the headlines on their work computers as they eat breakfast there, the rationale for massacring trees to produce a print edition seems less and less clear. Paper, ink, printing machines, and delivery costs are expensive. Without them, newspapers would be a lot more profitable. And as publications break more and more of their stories online (because the twenty-four-hour news cycle doesn't allow them to wait for the next morning's paper), the traditions of print and broadcast media will have to change.

The Old News Cycle Is Toast

On Monday, March 10, 2008, *The New York Times* published one of its biggest scoops of the year. It was juicy. Titillating. The editors who OK'd it were sure it would drive the day's news. But the scoop didn't appear in the morning's print edition, despite the little box in the top left corner of the front page noting that the stack of paper contained "All the news that's fit to print." Instead, a notice posted on *The New York Times*'s website at 2:00 P.M. announced that New York's then-governor Eliot Spitzer had been linked to a prostitution ring.

The Friday before, someone involved in the case had told reporter William Rashbaum that a New York official was being targeted by an investigation, but *The New York Times*' metro desk had to burn through a lot of shoe leather over the weekend figuring out who that official was. The newspaper put in calls to Spitzer's press office, which alerted the governor that something was going on. The story wasn't fully confirmed by the time the Monday paper went to print. But Spitzer canceled most of his Monday events, which alerted other media types that big news could be breaking. Holding the story until Tuesday's paper would have been too late. The only way to break the news as an exclusive was through the website. The *Times* did just that, got its scoop—and the story spread through the Internet faster than a Paris Hilton sex tape.

As the major news outlets have beefed up their online presence and started doing the regular updating that blogging demands, the news cycle has sped up exponentially.

In the really old days (say, thirty years ago), people would release information at 10:00 A.M. on a weekday, so it would first be on the news that evening. Then that news would appear in the next day's paper—with more analysis and quotes from people on the other side of the story. The advent of CNN, and then Fox News, MSNBC, etc., sped this up considerably. If you held a press conference announcing one thing, pundits who agreed and disagreed with you would be debating your version of events shortly afterward.

And blogs have shortened the news cycle even more. Now, if big news is announced at 10:00 A.M., it will be on everyone's website by 10:10—or faster. The blogs will start discussing it, batting back questions and new information. Glenn Reynolds (Instapundit) sometimes puts five new posts per hour up on his site. The time stamps on posts at *National Review*'s The Corner are rarely more than half an hour apart. Stories change quickly. For instance, after New School student commencement speaker Jean Rohe decided to preempt John McCain's speech to her graduating class by critiquing it (he repeated the stump speech he'd given at Jerry Falwell's Liberty University one week earlier), she wrote about her reasons for doing so on HuffPost at 6:59 P.M. on May 20, 2006. She reprinted her speech, which claimed, "The senator does not reflect the ideals upon which this university was founded." By 10:28 P.M. that same night, Mark Salter, a McCain aide, had written a lengthy response as a comment, concluding that "you might look back on the day of your graduation and your discourtesy to a good and honest man with a little shame and the certain knowledge that it is very unlikely any of you will ever posses . . . one small fraction of the character of John McCain."

The whole blog-speed vortex can be a bit dizzying if the "big news" is ever about you. We can only imagine what March 2008 was like for Ashley Youmans, a.k.a. "Ashley Alexandra Dupré," a.k.a. "Kristen," the high-priced prostitute Spitzer had been cavorting with. The day her identity went public, her MySpace page was viewed 4.7 million times. Her former teacher Gerald Basiak became a minor celebrity because he gave an interview about her to New Jersey's *Asbury Park Press*. All this information, including the music single Ashley/Kristen shrewdly chose to release, became fodder for wagging tongues. When the blogosphere lights up, the flame burns bright.

But it also burns out quickly. You don't hear much about Kristen anymore. Frankly, you don't hear much about Spitzer, either (though Spitzer may want some advice from Martha Stewart, whose blog postings following her release from prison made her more accessible to fans and likeable to the press, thus saving her name—and her brand). In the blog-era news cycle, being first is about minutes—and then moving on.

Woodward, Bernstein, and YOUR NAME HERE: Everyone Can Be a Reporter

Along with the decline of print, whenever you get journalists together, they talk about the pros and cons of professionalizing the job. Once, journalism was something you did. Now, you study it. Many grizzled veterans of the chain-smoking newsroom days think this is ridiculous. They were appalled when people started getting college degrees in journalism. The idea of a master's degree in journalism, or, God forbid, a PhD, makes them apoplectic. Don't bother, they growl as they stub out their cigarettes in the ashtrays outside the front door. Instead, go cover city council meetings for two years, or ride with cops on the night shift. That will teach you more about journalism than sitting in a classroom somewhere.

It's a romantic notion. But ever since the days of Deep Throat, journalism has seemed like a "cool" job. If you dig up a good enough story, Dustin Hoffman or Robert Redford might play you in the movie. Whenever a job is deemed "cool," more people haggle to get hired than there are positions available. This is doubly true in the face of declining advertising dollars and layoffs. Consequently, young reporters look for anything to give them a leg up on the competition. Advanced degrees are an obvious option (though not a foolproof one—the Cox Center's Annual Survey of Journalism and Mass Communication Graduates found that 76.2 percent of bachelor's degree recipients received at least one job offer; 72.2 percent of master's degree recipients did).

But blogs are turning this notion of an elite, degreed priesthood of journalists on its head. In the blogosphere, anyone can be a reporter. Anyone can find a story and put it out there for the world to read. Sometimes these citizen reporters like Mayhill Fowler break real news. But even when a blogger is writing about her personal everyday life, she still expects to be heard. And oftentimes, she will be.

If you think about it, this is a pretty revolutionary concept. Given the professionalizing of journalism, it's no surprise that journalists don't look exactly like America. They are more likely to be white; according to a 2008 American Society of Newspaper Editors survey, just 13.5 percent of journalists at daily newspapers were minorities (about a third of Americans are). Just 37 percent were women (compared to a fairly even split in the total population). Journalists are more likely to be from middle-class, professional backgrounds than other Americans. In many of the tributes following *Meet the Press* host Tim Russert's death, journalists took pains to point out that he was the son of a garbage collector. Of course, this seems like a foreign occupation to Russert's media colleagues.

We won't claim that blogging has opened up the conversation

Blogging for "Everymom"

What I like most [about blogging] is the ability to get my thoughts and opinions out into the world. I think this is especially valuable to stay-at-home-moms because we're pretty much invisible to the larger society. For example, early one morning I wrote a post about the two office supply superstores—Staples and Office Depot—I visited in my quest to buy a laptop. That's just what was on my mind. Imagine my surprise when my site meter indicated hits were coming in from Google Finance. My post had been linked to the Office Depot stock information page on GF. Yikes. Even though I'm no longer a stay-at-home mom, I still see myself as a sort of "everymom" just blogging from her basement late at night or before the kids wake up. In 2008, I've been interviewed for articles in national newspapers and magazines and been invited on fancy press-like junkets. Me—the mom blogging from her basement!

—KIM MOLDOFSKY, AUTHOR OF HORMONE-COLORED DAYS BLOG AND BLOGGER FOR PARENTCENTER

universally. Few folks in, say, Zimbabwe have access to the Internet. Even in America, if you don't own a computer or don't have the time to get to a library because you're working two jobs, blogging will be difficult. But since starting a blog is easier than getting hired at *The Washington Post*, the barriers that keep folks out of journalism have been dramatically lowered. And as people become used to having their say, they expect their community newspapers and television stations to listen to them.

Smart news outlets are opening themselves up to citizen reporters, like we did with our OffTheBus project. These citizen reporters don't necessarily want to enter the professional track of journalism, but they do like telling stories. As we were writing this, one Florida television station announced plans to hand out video cameras to twenty citizen journalists and pay them $20 for each video clip the station aired. The rationale was that twenty

It's Not Just Average Joes: Rich and Famous Bloggers

- **Paris Hilton's MySpace page (www.myspace.com/parishilton) takes on items printed in the *New York Post* ("I'm sick of Page Six and other gossip sites printing completely false stories").**
- **Rosie O'Donnell took her spat with Donald Trump into the blogosphere, calling him a "pimp" and "the comb over" at Rosie.com (incidentally, Donald Trump also keeps a blog).**
- **Carl Icahn started The Icahn Report online to criticize bad management decisions.**
- **Martha Stewart's The Martha Blog touts good household decisions.**
- **Humorist Dave Barry updates his *Miami Herald* blog multiple times per day.**
- **Can't touch this URL: MC Hammer already has it (mchammer.blogspot.com).**
- **David Beckham blogs once a week on his eponymous website with news about life in LA and pictures of him looking . . . hot.**

additional cameras would allow the news station to cover parts of the community it had neglected. *Time* magazine now solicits reader questions for its weekly profile subject. When collapsing cranes suddenly became a trend story in spring, 2008, *The New York Times* invited nearby readers to submit photos and information.

With so much competition, this should, in theory, put pressure on existing columnists and journalists to make sure they're on top of their game. We can all speak truth to power. What professional journalists have to offer that justifies their incomes should be expertise. As more people become citizen reporters, the rationale for employing mediocre professional journalists will fade. Indeed, not long ago, Pasadenanow.com announced that it would outsource reporting on city council meetings to reporters in India (since the council meetings are broadcast online). But star reporters will still command big bucks for their articles and books. You can read plenty of Barbara Ehrenreich's musings free of charge on the Internet (on her website and on HuffPost). But people still buy *Nickel and Dimed: On (Not) Getting By in America* hoping to get a little more of her voice and her reporting. There's no going back to the days when there were people with press passes, and everyone else.

 ## YOU'LL NEVER *NOT* BLOG IN THIS TOWN AGAIN

ALEXANDER REMINGTON, *WASHINGTON POST* EDITORIAL ASSISTANT AND HUFFPOST BLOGGER

I wrote a piece about Sarah Silverman, and in the course of taking her to task for having a shtick with a limited shelf life—I like her, but I think she needs to branch out or she'll just disappear—I made a negative throwaway remark about her performance in Jeff Garlin's *I Want Someone to Eat Cheese With,* calling her basically nothing but a sex object. The piece got a lot of comments, including one from Garlin himself, taking me to task and saying I never even saw the movie. Thrilled and righteously indignant, I wrote back to say I actually *had* seen it, and what's more I thought her character was thinly written. He never responded, but I was on cloud nine for days. (I pissed off a Hollywood director! I'm on top of the world!)

The Definition of News Is Expanding

The defining feature of print and broadcast media is limited space. Unless your readers have magnifying glasses, the front page of a newspaper can hold a few thousand words at most. Consequently, editors and reporters have long served a gatekeeper function, choosing what to put in that limited space. The old saying "If it bleeds, it leads" is instructive—if you have limited space, you have to make choices, and violent, bloody events tend to win. If there is a major accident in the mall parking lot in your town, it will take precedence over a feature piece about a local pastor's work in the community. The problem is, these accidents, food scares, political conflicts, and the like keep bumping that pastor off the front page until Easter, when you've got a religion news hook. This presents a distorted view of what's actually going on in the community. Presumably, only a half-dozen people were affected by that grisly mall parking lot accident. The local pastor may have affected thousands of people in far more profound ways.

Since the blogosphere is not subject to the tyranny of space, the pastor and the mall parking lot accident can exist side by side. So can slow-burn stories like, say, the fact that the infant mortality rate for African-American babies is much higher than for white babies. There is no one event to hook such a story to, so media outlets looking for the bleeding lede won't lead with it. But blogs can. Blogs can cover smaller stories that a newspaper or TV news station would never see fit to—a poetry reading in a local café, for instance, or (from a widely read HuffPost blog) Jamie Lee Curtis's musings on how she learned to sew a hem in school but kids don't study home economics anymore. If it matters to somebody, it will find its audience.

Blogging can also resurrect stories that seem to have come and

FIND YOUR NET NICHE
MARCIA YERMAN, JOURNALIST AND HUFFPOST BLOGGER

Blogging gives me the opportunity to write about content that is too often overlooked by the mainstream media. My area of focus is women's issues, culture, and the arts. Having established myself in this niche, people often contact me with stories about events, forums, or cultural happenings that otherwise would remain under the radar.

gone. That's what happened with the late 2006/early 2007 story about how the Bush administration had fired several U.S. attorneys, seemingly for political reasons. In December, Josh Marshall of Talking Points Memo linked to an *Arkansas Democrat-Gazette* story about one such attorney being replaced. In the old days, that might have been the end of it. The firing happened, it was reported on, nothing more to see here, move on. But Marshall followed up with reports on other U.S. attorney replacements he had read about and then asked his readers to report if any U.S. attorneys in their districts had lost their jobs. Soon, Talking Points Memo readers had pieced together a story of a politicized Justice Department that *every* media outlet had to cover.

Because there is no tyranny of space, in the blog world, the news not only doesn't have to matter to the gatekeepers, it doesn't even have to be new. Bloggers put whatever they want out there, and if enough people start paying attention to it, it becomes news to the mainstream media. It's a world of potential second chances and a world where the past doesn't stay buried if people see a reason to unbury it. **As Jay Rosen memorably observed, the blogosphere has become the "court of appeals in news judgment."**

BLOGGING LETS CONTENT BE KING

JIM MOORE, EMMY-WINNING TV NEWS CORRESPONDENT AND HUFFPOST BLOGGER

My second book, *Bush's War for Reelection: Iraq, the White House, and the People,* involved the first extensive analysis and criticism of Judy Miller of *The New York Times* and how she failed as a journalist. I interviewed Miller, her colleagues, several officers in Iraq, and numerous people within and without the military, intelligence agencies, and the U.S. government to get a sense of how she got information and how it was used. Unfortunately, my publisher was compelled to release the book in the midst of a flurry of new publications by former White House officials and Ambassador Joe Wilson's book about the attack on his secret-agent wife. My book, in addition to detailing Miller's failings, also included the culmination of more than a decade's work researching George Bush's mysterious tenure in the Texas Air National Guard. My findings led to the national controversy on the president's service. But virtually no one read my book. However, I later pulled out the chapters on Judy Miller and published them on The Huffington Post. I constantly get e-mails and phone calls and see numerous references to this work. It seems to be virtually everywhere; I rarely get interviewed without someone asking me about the research, and although it was first published in my obscure book, it is always referred to as "your Huffington Post piece on Judy Miller." The web and blogging gave that work some life and value and kept it from disappearing into obscurity. This is what a writer hopes for . . . almost as much as a fat royalty check.

Getting Reality Fact-Checked

One of the most exciting ways bloggers are shaping the media is through their work as an army of fact-checkers and, more broadly, reality-checkers.

Old-fashioned fact-checking is a dying art. Some publications, such as *The New Yorker,* still employ people to go back through their reporters' work and make sure every little detail is right. Calling them thorough would be an understatement. Experts contacted in the fact-checking process speak of being on the phone for twenty minutes gauging the accuracy of a throwaway line. But this kind of fact-checking is a rarity. This is a problem because to err is human. And reporters are definitely human.

In the past, victims of reporting inaccuracies—or even misperceptions—had little recourse. When media outlets got something wrong, they might print a correction or have the anchor apologize on air once the error came to light. But anyone calling the newspaper to report an error or grievance would have to wait to see their concerns addressed and would not know if other people were also calling.

Now, of course, if you see a misrepresentation in a story, most websites, including ours, let you post a comment on that exact same story. Everyone who reads the story will see it. Because blogs are updated constantly, an error can be corrected as soon as it's noticed.

More broadly, though, bloggers and their readers aren't just fact-checking stories. They're also taking over the reality-checking function long served by institutions such as the *Columbia Journalism Review.* The handful of publications that cover the media ask their readers to step back and look at how stories were presented. Have newspapers been quoting too many of the same pundits? How are people with conservative or liberal leanings identified? These are important questions. But with weeks or months passing between a story and a critique appearing (at least in the past), the criticism was less than immediately useful. And, given that journalism reviews are often published by journalism schools that produce the same kinds of people who become journalists in the first place, these reviews can be subject to similar biases as the media themselves.

Now we can all be journalism critics. And not only can we comment on the reporting, we can comment on the quotes in the reporting and how people choose to present themselves. The obligatory quote from the congressman will no longer stand, uncommented, if there's more to the story than what he's saying. Blogs are increasing the chances that total BS will be exposed.

How Your Blog Can Have Impact in a Post–Mass Media World

The days of everyone watching network news and reading the local newspaper are long gone. In the face of declining ad revenue and the rise of the democratic, constantly updated blogosphere, mainstream media outlets are trying to figure out what they can offer their audiences. What does it take to make it today?

We'd say the same thing it takes to make it as a blogger: offering content you can't get anywhere else, presented in a compelling way. Good media outlets focus on their core competencies. These are the things you do best, that other people can't do as well.

Phil Meyer, the UNC journalism professor, identifies these newspaper core competencies as the kind of deep, investigative reporting and compelling feature writing that attracts "the hardcore news junkie." These well-educated people do tend to be attractive to advertisers, so that's one way to survive. Another is for newspapers to realize that "it won't matter who reads them—what they produce will be diffused by bloggers." In that world, it is the content that matters, not the number of eyeballs that look at your

THE MEDIA LISTENED TO THIS VET'S VOICE

BRANDON FRIEDMAN, AUTHOR OF *THE WAR I ALWAYS WANTED*
AND HUFFPOST BLOGGER

In the grand scheme of things, I've made more of an impact other times, but when I broke the story on VetVoice about how pro–Iraq War congressman Patrick McHenry (R-NC) had endangered American lives in Iraq, that was the most satisfying. After a visit to Iraq, a very self-satisfied McHenry posted a video on his congressional website in which he proudly described the battle damage caused by a missile strike in the Green Zone. In doing so, he violated a military policy put in place to protect Americans in combat zones. After I wrote about it, the traditional media picked it up, as did McHenry's primary opponent. The story clearly got under the skin of McHenry and his opponent even used it against him by turning it into a television ad. McHenry ultimately won his primary, but I doubt he'll be showing off in combat zones again anytime soon.

product on any given morning. To survive in that world, mainstream media outlets might end up being supported by foundations, wealthy individuals, or others who have an interest in good content rather than high profits. There's some historical precedent for this. The popes of the Middle Ages and the Italian patrons of the Renaissance funded top-quality art without asking that all sculptures feature ads somewhere on the torso. A steady stream of portraits often sufficed.

We don't know how this will all shake out. But we do know that in the blogosphere, as we all add our own critiques and new information, something starts to emerge that looks more like the truth. We've been fascinated to read studies showing that asking more and more people a question (e.g., "How tall is the Tower of London?") and averaging their answers yields something closer to the truth than asking one person alone. This is—in a nutshell—how the blogosphere is reshaping the media. In the past, voices were necessarily limited. So the information we received was limited as well. Now, as everyone feels free to contribute, we get a clearer picture of reality. If the function of the media is to inform, and to get the real story, then we'd say blogs are shaping the media in a positive way. That's true even if come 2043, we'll have to use something else to line our birdcages.

BRINGING MORE VOICES UNDER THE CYBER-TENT

KERRY TRUEMAN, COFOUNDER OF THE EATING LIBERALLY BLOG AND HUFFPOST BLOGGER

A woman in Sioux Falls named Jen e-mailed me to say, "I love reading your posts—it is like having a good friend who does all the research on stuff I care about and then sends me funny notes about them!!"

I thanked her for the feedback. In a follow-up e-mail, Jen told me a bit about her life:

I am currently working a pretty unfortunate "in-between" job that involves driving too far, watching people buy China-made crap they don't need, and a boss who insists on listening to right-wing talk radio . . . in other words, lots of things that get me down.

She thanked me for inspiring her to read Bill McKibben's *Deep Economy,* which helped galvanize her to make some changes a few months later:

I have to tell you that you inspired me to find a job closer to home, and one that didn't involve selling people more crap they didn't need . . . I start tomorrow at a job that is close enough that I can walk or ride my bike—yay!! I was tired of listening to myself bitch so now I'll be somewhere within walking distance—I can come home for lunch and visit my dog, and I know there will be no Repub talk radio.

Knowing that I helped to lift one fellow liberal out of the sonic cesspool of Limbaugh, O'Reilly, et al., sustains me when blogger burnout starts to set in.

PART III

THE HUFFINGTON POST RESOURCE SECTION

THE HUFFINGTON POST BLOGROLL

GLOSSARY OF BLOGGING TERMS

WEBSITE RESOURCE LIST

BEST OF THE HUFFPOST BLOGS

THE HUFFINGTON POST BLOGROLL

Being a great blogger means reading (and linking to) other blogs. If you decide you really like one, consider putting it on your blogroll. With any luck, that's a favor your new blogroll buddy will soon return. Here is a list of forty-nine sites we've put on our blogroll and why we think you should check them out.

BOING BOING—boingboing.net
Since launching in 2000, this offbeat "Directory of Wonderful Things" has become one of the most popular sites in the world. It features an entertaining stream of geek-oriented oddities and pop-culture ephemera and an antiauthority posture, making it both a pioneer of Internet culture and one of the all-time great diversions on the web.

BUZZMACHINE—buzzmachine.com
The prolific Jeff Jarvis (founding editor of *Entertainment Weekly*, former television critic for *People*, current columnist for *The Guardian*) may be an Old Media titan, but his savvy, informed take on the latest Internet developments is definitely the work of a man who gets New Media.

THE CONSUMERIST—consumerist.com

Nothing annoys the American shopping public more than feeling they are getting screwed by companies—and capitalism—which is why this site, where "shoppers bite back," has become the premier clearinghouse for consumer angst.

CROOKS AND LIARS—crooksandliars.com

Founded by professional sax and flute player (and HuffPost contributor) John Amato, this immensely popular political blog uses a heavy dose of video clips to expose the unending stream of "spin" deployed by politicians and TV talking heads.

THE DAILY DISH—andrewsullivan.theatlantic.com

One of the first mainstream journalists to make his way into the blogosphere (he's been online since 2000), Andrew Sullivan holds a wealth of contradictory positions (antitax, social liberal, prowar) that defy partisan categories. That makes him one of the most unorthodox and illuminating voices on the web and one of the few commentators who can ruffle feathers on the left and right alike.

DAILY INTELLIGENCER—nymag.com/daily/intel

New York magazine's blog holds its own in the crowded field of clever, Manhattan-centric news sites (see Gawker). Like the magazine itself, it offers a seamless mix of serious news and diverting gossip that's well suited to the everything-goes world of the web.

DAILY KOS—dailykos.com

The true epicenter for online liberal activists, or a.k.a. the "Netroots," Markos Moulitsas's constantly buzzing collaborative site has become a force in the Democratic Party. Its discussion boards, group blogs, and political encyclopedia exemplify the impassioned, if not always polite, debate that fuels the blogosphere.

DEADLINE HOLLYWOOD DAILY—deadlinehollywooddaily.com
Longtime journalist and *LA Weekly* columnist Nikki Finke's site, an extension of her take-no-prisoners "Deadline Hollywood" column, has become essential reading for those following the ins and outs of the infotainment industry. She's got expertise, 24/7 reporting, and unapologetic sass.

DEALBOOK—dealbook.blogs.nytimes.com
Among the major newspapers, *The New York Times* has been the most ambitious at developing blogs across the various sections of its newspaper. Its business news blog, edited by the prolific Andrew Ross Sorkin, is one of its best as well as an essential resource for those trying to keep tabs on the wild ride of the marketplace.

DEALBREAKER—dealbreaker.com
Dealbreaker (launched by Gawker alum Elizabeth Spiers) takes a tabloid approach to the business world, passing along Wall Street gossip and commentary on financial industry personalities in equal proportions.

DEFAMER—defamer.com
Few sites do snark better than those started by Gawker Media, and few places are easier targets of derision than Hollywood. So it's not surprising that the commentary on this LA gossip blog, which takes aim at the entertainment industry and its stars, is relentlessly caustic.

DLISTED—dlisted.com

The phrase "Be Very Afraid" adorns the top of blogger Michael K's savagely biting celebrity gossip site. It's sound advice for any of the tabloid standbys who are on the receiving end of his scathing commentary, which he files at the staggering rate of over twenty posts a day.

DRUDGE REPORT—drudgereport.com

Whether or not Matt Drudge's site truly fits the definition of a blog, its idiosyncratic mix of lo-fi design, news aggregation, and tabloid instincts hasn't lost any of its appeal. He still snags scoops and influences news coverage a decade after his publishing of a rumor about Bill Clinton and a woman named Monica made him a media sensation.

ECOFABULOUS—ecofabulous.com

Green is the new blog, you might say, and this particular site—where "sustainable" meets "sexy"—is one of the best guides to sorting through the (thankfully) burgeoning array of green products and services.

EPICENTER—blog.wired.com/business

It should be no surprise to learn that leading techno-culture magazine *Wired*—which produces a number of popular and informative blogs (check out Threat Level, Danger Room, Gadget Lab)—covers its neighbors in Silicon Valley much better than most.

ESCHATON—eschatonblog.com

Former economics professor Duncan Black's popular politics blog, which he writes under the name Atrios, delivers short, punchy critiques aimed squarely at the GOP and the mainstream media. Be prepared for edgy humor (e.g., "wanker of the day").

FIREDOGLAKE — firedoglake.com
A hard-nosed progressive site founded by film producer Jane Hamsher and written as a group blog, the site made a splash during the Scooter Libby trial by using six rotating bloggers to produce what *The New York Times* called the "fullest, fastest public report available" of the trial. Mainstream journalists started following the site themselves to learn what was going on.

FIRST READ — firstread.msnbc.msn.com
MSNBC is a great place to get your daily headline news fix, but for hard-core politics junkies, the network's First Read blog is an even better destination. Headed by NBC's encyclopedic political director Chuck Todd, it features even-tempered, expert analysis of the day's news.

FOOTNOTED — footnoted.org
Started by financial journalist Michelle Leder, this investigative blog combs through company SEC filings looking for the juicy details hidden inside (check out the site's helpful guide to interpreting filings).

GAWKER — gawker.com
This eponymous flagship site of New Media mogul Nick Denton's blog empire (see Wonkette, Defamer, etc.) may have lost some of its edge now that the success of its snarky outsider's take on the media industry has made it part of the establishment. Still, its gossipy chronicling of the ups and downs of media personalities,

though more focused on celebs than industry insiders these days, remains hilarious, unsparing, and dead-on.

GRIDSKIPPER — gridskipper.com
Part of the trendy Curbed blog network, this global urban travel blog caters to the relatively young and mobile. It's the perfect guide for those who aspire to cosmopolitan jet-setting (the editors "moor" themselves in the Hamptons for the summer) and the place to read about the latest hot spots for breakfasting in Sydney, shopping in Tokyo, and partying in LA.

INFORMED COMMENT — juancole.com
Juan Cole, a professor of modern Middle Eastern history at the University of Michigan, has been blogging about Iraq since 2002. His wide-ranging knowledge of the region (as well as his strong criticisms of the Bush administration) has made him one of the most popular and respected commentators on foreign policy.

INHABITAT — inhabitat.com
This visually striking blog, founded by NYC designer Jill Fehrenbacher, proves that sustainability and stylishness go hand in hand. It chronicles the latest trends and innovations in technology and design, looking at such topics as green building, renewable energy, and eco-friendly products.

INSTAPUNDIT — pajamasmedia.com/instapundit
University of Tennessee law professor and self-described libertarian Glenn Reynolds has been referred to as the Blogfather— he was one of the genre's first breakout stars. His learned, opinionated, politics-heavy site remains one of the most popular on the web.

JUST JARED — justjared.buzznet.com

This pop-culture news and gossip blog is heavy on colorful photos and surprisingly light on off-color commentary (see Perez Hilton for that). It offers a gentler embrace of its celebrity subjects and a greater focus on trend spotting than many similarly themed blogs.

KAUSFILES — slate.com/id/2065132/landing/1

Back in 1999, the inimitable Mickey Kaus was among the first wave of mainstream journalists to embrace the then nascent world of blogging. His "mostly political" blog (hosted by *Slate*) is predictably unpredictable in its often contrarian take on current events. He's also a cofounder of the popular "dia-vlog" Blogging heads.tv.

KOTTKE.ORG — kottke.org

For over a decade now, pioneering blogger and web designer Jason Kottke has been one of the premier arbiters of interesting reading on the Internet. His simple, old-school-looking site keeps tabs on what's new and intriguing across a wide, and impressively esoteric, array of subjects.

LA OBSERVED — laobserved.com

Former *Los Angeles Times* journalist Kevin Roderick has been called the West-Coast Romenesko (whose blog is listed below), and his popular LA-focused blog is indeed a go-to place for keeping tabs on the city's media scene, as well as its politics. Rare for the blogosphere, he keeps his attitude in check.

MARC AMBINDER—marcambinder.theatlantic.com

Marc Ambinder, a veteran of political news blogs at The Hotline and ABC, calls his current one at *The Atlantic* a "reported blog on politics." This commitment to producing original reporting alongside opinion makes his a must-read site.

MATTHEW YGLESIAS—yglesias.thinkprogress.org

Online since 2002, Yglesias recently moved his popular political blog to Think Progress after having made stops along the way at a who's who of progressive politics sites—*The American Prospect*, Talking Points Memo, *The Atlantic*. He is one of the sharpest and most outspoken thinkers in the blogosphere.

MEDIA MATTERS—mediamatters.org

Since its founding in 2004, this nonprofit watchdog and vigilant rapid-responder to "conservative misinformation throughout the media" has been posting judicious rebuttals to whoppers or smears dispatched by repeat offenders Rush Limbaugh, Michael Savage, Fox News, and countless others.

THE MEDIA MOB—observer.com/themediamob

Unlike Gawker or *New York* magazine's Daily Intel, the *Observer*'s media blog serves its news straight—it goes light on the snide and leaves the celebrities and politicians aside—and its trio of reporters delivers an informative and focused take on the industry.

PAIDCONTENT—paidcontent.org

Rafat Ali's news blog reports on the intricacies of the online media business and has become a site of record for those trying to figure out the economics behind a future dominated by digital content.

PEREZ HILTON—perezhilton.com

Love him or detest him (or both), the notoriously shameless celebrity gossip Perez (real name Mario Lavandeira) wields an undeniable influence due to his mischievous and occasionally scurrilous blog. He doodles obscenities on celebrity photos, outs closeted stars, and engages in an unleashed display of self-promotion that has made him a celeb in his own right.

THE PLANK—blogs.tnr.com/tnr/blogs/the_plank

The New Republic's political blog, much like similar ones found at *The Nation* and *The American Prospect*, features the kind of astute analysis and intense debate of ideas that one can find in these prominent liberal magazines (but produced at blogosphere speed).

POLITICAL RADAR—blogs.abcnews.com/politicalradar

Even though people may not tune in to network news shows as much as they used to, many can turn to abcnews.com's political news blog, which is complemented by Jake Tapper's Political Punch. Great reporting from the field.

POPSUGAR—popsugar.com

Unlike many celebrity-oriented sites, this blog (one of fifteen sites in the Sugar Publishing network) forgoes cattiness for a tone that's amused and easygoing. It offers a lighthearted take on style and beauty along the lines of a mainstream women's magazine.

RADAR ONLINE—radaronline.com

The online-wing of the oft-relaunched pop culture magazine is not alone among New York blogs in bringing an irreverent intelligence to the media and celebrity worlds, but the site's ability to break stories, along with its wit, makes it well worth the time.

ROMENESKO—poynter.org/column.asp?id=45
Jim Romenesko's eponymous journalism blog, which is backed by the nonprofit Poynter Institute, is a one-man media-news institution. Part watchdog and part industry gossip, its wide scope makes it mandatory reading for those who care about the Fourth Estate.

THE SARTORIALIST—thesartorialist.blogspot.com
Fashion veteran Scott Schuman has taken a simple concept—a collection of photos showcasing various styles that have caught his eye on the street—and transformed it into one of the most enjoyable, not to mention popular, fashion blogs on the web.

SILICON ALLEY INSIDER—alleyinsider.com
Edited by Henry Blodget, this blog's mix of insider news and informed commentary is essential reading for those who are looking to stay up to speed on developments in New Media business, particularly in New York City (Silicon Alley refers to an area with a large concentration of New Media companies in downtown Manhattan).

BEN SMITH—politico.com/blogs/bensmith
When it came to covering the 2008 election, few bloggers consistently produced more scoops or better up-to-the-minute analysis of the latest twists in the campaign than Politico's Ben Smith. The site has quickly become a major player in the world of political journalism.

TALKING POINTS MEMO—talkingpointsmemo.com

Joshua Marshall's site (TPM to its readers) has become the gold standard of online political journalism, having shown time and time again that a small team of determined bloggers can break big stories. Proof: TPM's relentless pursuit of the U.S. attorney firing scandal story helped lead to Alberto Gonzales resigning and Marshall becoming the first blogger to win the prestigious George Polk journalism award.

THINK PROGRESS—thinkprogress.org

Launched in 2005 as the daily blog of the Center for American Progress Action Fund, this well-researched and hard-nosed progressive site pushes back against the excesses of right-wing misinformation and corruption.

TMZ—tmz.com

No one practices the art (if you can call it that) of celebrity stalking quite like this massively popular, AOL-backed site. Its staff churns out a nonstop parade of news, photos, videos, and "exclusives" that is enough to satiate even the most obsessive fan of celebrity gossip. TMZ makes traditional tabloids look quaint by comparison.

TREEHUGGER—treehugger.com

The blog that aims to bring the ethos of sustainable living to the masses (and prove that it's not the big sacrifice people think) is the ultimate hub for news, consumer info, and advice on living the green life. It is consistently one of the top twenty blogs on Technorati.

TVNEWSER—mediabistro.com/tvnewser

Mediabistro's blog about the TV news industry, founded by wunderkind journalist and current NYT employee Brian Stelter is one of the best sources for tracking who's up in the ratings, who's on the way out the door, and who just said something totally insane on CNN.

THE WEALTH REPORT—blogs.wsj.com/wealth

Everyone likes reading about the lives and lifestyles of the rich (admit it), and when it comes to reporting on the latest developments in the world of the wealthy (sample headline: "The $300 Million Mystery Yacht Revealed"), this blog, written by *The Wall Street Journal*'s Robert Frank, has what you want.

WONKETTE—wonkette.com

The blog that made its name covering Beltway politics with equal parts intelligence, sarcasm, irony, and profanity—and made its founding editor, Ana Marie Cox, a media star—may no longer be part of the Gawker Media empire, but it's hard to imagine a funnier take on the political scene.

GLOSSARY OF BLOGGING TERMS

Terms to help you talk the talk so you can blog the blog. All are referred to in this book.

blog—derived from the term "web log"; regularly updated account of events on a website, commonly listed in reverse chronological order

blogger—someone who writes blog posts

blogging—writing a blog post

blogosphere—the collective community of blogs

blogroll—list of links to other blogs or websites, often featured in a sidebar on a blog

CAPTCHA—acronym for "Completely Automated Public Turing Test to tell Computers and Humans Apart." Usually requires user to type squiggly characters that are hard for a computer to identify. Used to thwart spam-bots

commentor—someone who leaves remarks on a blog post (some people spell it "commenter")

comments—remarks left on a blog post

copyright—ownership of an intellectual property (e.g., an article or photo)

fair use—the right to use parts of copyrighted materials for certain purposes, such as criticism

header—distinct logo on top of your website

hit—browser's request for information from a server

HTML—stands for Hyper Text Markup Language; used to write web pages

keyword—a word or phrase a user might search for

links—enable a reader to open another webpage with one click

moderate—to monitor your comments (either before they go up on your blog or after the fact)

page views—metric for counting every time a visitor opens a page on your blog

photolog—blog with a focus on visual images

podcasts—digital sound clips to be played over the Internet

post—an entry on a blog

RSS—stands for "Really Simple Syndication"; a web feed format for syndicating your blog

search engine—program that turns up most relevant websites based on keywords

search engine optimization (SEO)—editing your website to come up higher on a search for any given keyword

sidebar—information other than a blog post on blog page, usually off to the side

spam—unwanted advertising posts or comments left on your blog

tags—keywords used to identify and help collect similar posts

template—basic background of a blog

title—headline of a blog post

troll—a disruptive commenter bent on making trouble on a site

unique visitors—metric for measuring the number of different people who visited your site during a given period of time

vlogs—video logs, a.k.a. blog posts containing video

WEBSITE RESOURCE LIST

We've gathered open-source software, lists, tools, and more that will be indispensible to a successful blog. We suggest you bookmark these sites—along with The Huffington Post, of course.

Alexa (alexa.com)—Company that measures traffic on websites

A List Apart (alistapart.com)—Long-running site that's a good resource for info on web design and development

Amazon Associates (https://affiliate-program.amazon.com)—Referral program; if a visitor buys products through the Amazon links you host on your site, you get a referral fee

Blogger (https://www.blogger.com)—Free blogging service owned by Google

Daily Blog Tips (dailyblogtips.com)—Site full of helpful tips for improving your blog

Delicious (delicious.com)—Site that allows you to bookmark your favorite websites and share the list with your friends

Digg (digg.com)—Social news site where users vote on their favorite stories by "digging" them

Dosh Dosh (doshdosh.com)—Blog that provides info on Internet marketing and making money online

Facebook (facebook.com)—Popular social networking site

Google AdSense (https://www.google.com/adsense)—Program that matches ads to your site's content; pays based on clicks

Google Alerts (google.com/alerts)—Service that e-mails you a link every time your name, or the name of your blog, is mentioned on another site

Google Analytics (google.com/analytics)—Service that offers free visitor tracking and analysis of traffic on your blog

LiveJournal (livejournal.com)—Free blogging service owned by SUP

Mashable (mashable.com)—Popular blog about social networking

Movable Type (movabletype.org)—Open-source blog publishing service from Six Apart

MySpace (myspace.com)—Popular social networking site, especially with musicians

NewsTrust (newstrust.net)—Social news site where members vote on their favorite stories

Nielsen Online Ratings (nielsen-netratings.com)—Measures traffic for websites, much like Nielsen does for TV channels

Problogger (problogger.net)—Blog that offers lots of helpful tips for developing your blogging skills and making money on your blog

Reddit (reddit.com)—Social news site where users vote on their favorite stories

Site Meter (sitemeter.com)—Tool for measuring traffic on your blog

StatCounter (statcounter.com)—Tool for measuring traffic on your blog

StumbleUpon (stumbleupon.com)—Network where users can rate web pages and discover sites that fit their interests

Technorati (technorati.com)—Blog search engine

Top Tut (toptut.com)—Blog about web design and development, with reviews of web hosting services

Tumblelogs (tumblr.com)—Short-form blogs, ideal for multi-media posting

Twitter (twitter.com)—Microblogging service that allows users to send updates via text-based messages

TypePad (typepad.com)—Paid blog publishing service owned by Six Apart

Webby Awards (webbyawards.com)—Annual awards ceremony honoring all kinds of Internet properties

WordPress (wordpress.org)—Open-source software for online publishing; company also offers free blog hosting service

Yahoo! Buzz (buzz.yahoo.com)—Site that allows users to vote for their favorite stories

Yahoo! Publisher Network (publisher.yahoo.com)—Like Google AdSense, pays you for clicks on ads you host on your site

BEST OF THE HUFFPOST BLOGS

Since our launch, HuffPost has published over 50,000 blog posts—so trying to pick out a limited collection of the best of them is an impossible task. So we didn't even try. Instead, we gathered together a tasty sampling of some of the more memorable posts that have appeared on our site over the last three-and-a-half years. Some capture a moment in time, and some are timeless; some are funny while some are deadly serious—but all of them are wonderful examples of terrific blogging.

BUSH: OF MOJO AND MACBETH
ARIANNA HUFFINGTON, POSTED 10.27.2005

More and more, Bush looks like a man who has reached the point of no return. Watching his robotic speech on Iraq this week, you got the sense his heart is no longer really in it. He seems defeated. Resigned. Running on empty.

It got me thinking of the way this happens in every great tragedy—Greek or Shakespearean. The moment arrives when we know that all is lost. For some reason, I keep thinking of Macbeth.

Macbeth's fatal deed—from which there was no return—was, of course, killing King Duncan ("Had I but died an hour before this chance, I had lived a blessed time"). Bush's fatal deed was invading Iraq. It led directly to Plamegate—an attempt to cover up the lies and deceptions used to sell an unnecessary war to the American people. It derailed the war on terror, increased anti-American feeling around the world, contributed to the soaring budget deficit, made us less safe here at home, and set the table for the disastrous mishandling of Hurricane Katrina.

In the Scottish play, Shakespeare perfectly captures the infinite weariness that sets in when you've reached the end of the road:

"Tomorrow, and tomorrow, and tomorrow, creeps in this petty pace from day to day, to the last syllable of recorded time; and all our yesterdays have lighted fools the way to dusty death."

Can you think of a better summation of the position Bush now finds himself in? There will be no legacy of endless Republican power. No grand remaking of the Middle East. No privatization of, well, everything. No shrinking the government. No superseding his father.

Instead, he's staggering toward his dusty political death—marking time until the last syllable of his recorded time in office in January 2009. Unless his last syllable comes sooner—with Pat Fitzgerald as his Macduff, running a dagger through the heart of his presidency and sending him off on an early permanent vacation at the Crawford ranch.

I imagine the mood in the Oval Office today is not dissimilar to that in Dunsinane Castle when a messenger arrives with news that (as prophesied by the three witches) the trees of Birnam Wood are advancing on Macbeth's castle, auguring his demise. The doomed king realizes that all is lost and, resigned, awaits his destiny. As Macbeth steeled himself for the arrival of the Birnam

Wood, Bush must be steeling himself for the arrival of Fitzgerald's indictments.

Out, out, brief candle!

 ## BOB WOODWARD, THE DUMB BLONDE OF AMERICAN JOURNALISM

ARIANNA HUFFINGTON, POSTED 11.28.2005

"I've spent my life," Bob Woodward told Larry King last week, "trying to find out what's really hidden, what's in the bottom of the barrel."

I found myself thinking about Woodward and his barrel-searching as I read Frank Rich's latest takedown of the administration's cover up of "wrongdoing in the executive branch between 9/11 and shock and awe":

Each day brings slam-dunk evidence that the doomsday threats marshaled by the administration to sell the war weren't, in Cheney-speak, just dishonest and reprehensible but also corrupt and shameless . . . The web of half-truths and falsehoods used to sell the war did not happen by accident; it was woven by design and then foisted on the public by a PR operation built expressly for that purpose in the White House.

During this time, Woodward was writing two books on the administration—*Bush at War* and *Plan of Attack*—and enjoyed unparalleled access to many of those guiding the aforementioned PR operation, including head shills Dick Cheney, Scooter Libby, and Andy Card.

So how come Woodward, supposedly the preeminent investigative reporter of our time, missed the biggest story of our time—a story that was taking place right under his nose?

Some would say it's because he's carrying water for the Bushies. I disagree. I think it's because he's the dumb blonde of American journalism, so awed by his proximity to power that he buys whatever he's being sold.

In her scathing 1996 essay in *The New York Review of Books*, Joan Didion criticized Woodward's reporting as marked by "a scrupulous passivity, an agreement to cover the story not as it is occurring but as it is presented, which is to say as it is manufactured."

And far from shying away from his reputation as a stenographer to the political stars, Woodward has embraced his inner bimbo and wears his "scrupulous passivity" as a badge of honor, proudly telling Larry King that his "method" means that "everyone in the end . . . pretty much gets their point of view out."

Woodward also told King: "I am strictly in the middle." The problem is, the truth isn't always in the middle; it's often located on the sidelines, or hiding in the shadows amidst the endless rush of detail Woodward so loves to fill his books with.

What Woodward fails to do again and again is connect the dots. He prefers to gather as many dots as he can, jam-pack his pages with them, and then let the little buggers hang out by themselves. Critical thinking that draws conclusions can be such a messy thing.

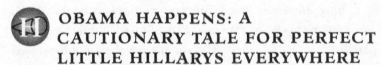

OBAMA HAPPENS: A CAUTIONARY TALE FOR PERFECT LITTLE HILLARYS EVERYWHERE

ARIANNA HUFFINGTON, POSTED 12.4.2006

Gather around, little ones, I have a story to tell you. It is a cautionary tale about a perfect little girl who had a seemingly perfect little plan.

The perfect girl was named Hillary and her plan was to become President of the United States. So, after joining the World's Most Exclusive Club, she set out to do everything her head—and her consultants—told her was right.

She learned the rules of the Club, and followed them closely. She reached across the aisle and brought home the bacon for her constituents back home.

She posed for smiling photo-ops with Bill Frist, Newt Gingrich, and Rick Santorum.

She backed a bill criminalizing flag burning, came out against violent video games, signed on to President Bush's missile defense plan, shifted her language on abortion, and became a bellicose backer of the war in Iraq—convinced that the country isn't ready for a female commander in chief who isn't a hawk.

She dutifully sharpened the points of her triangulation strategy, decorating her rhetoric in red-state-friendly shades. She was careful, oh so careful, and aimed to please—never saying anything that would get her in trouble.

She also quietly and methodically began building her campaign team—surrounding herself with a gaggle of advisers and consultants, raising millions of dollars (and lining up a top-flight national finance director to help her raise millions more), reaching out to power brokers in her home state, and sending out press releases through *The New York Times*.

She even hired a netroots pro to harness the energy of the Internet and help her win the favor of the blogosphere.

With Democrats on the rise, her perfect plan seemed to be working out perfectly.

And then suddenly, unexpectedly, came a rumbling in the distance. A rumbling caused by a boy named Barack. Indications are that before the year is out, Barack will officially be in.

All at once, a surge of enthusiasm and support for the boy named Barack is threatening to ruin all of the girl named Hillary's perfect plans—like sand castles being washed away by a rising tide.

So, my little ones, what is the lesson to be learned from this tale?

That you might as well speak your mind and do what is in your heart because you never know what waits around the corner— what unforeseen forces are headed your way.

As the poet tells us, the best-laid plans of mice and men—and perfect little girls—often go awry. And, man oh man, are they ever going awry for Hillary.

Well, you know what they say: Obama Happens.

GETTING TO THE DIRTY BOTTOM OF DAVID VITTER

CHRIS KELLY, POSTED 7.13.2007

While everyone is running around calling David Vitter a hypocrite, for the way his faith and politics ran counter to his private life, remember: Jesus hung out with prostitutes, too.

I went to a parochial school, and David Vitter has made my faith stronger than ever. Our creed tells us we're born bad, and it's a daily struggle just to not get an erotic massage, or five.

He proves Saint Augustine's point.

That's one of the main problems in our clash of cultures with the Muslim world. They don't believe in original sin. And there are a lot of things you can say about a sin like calling a whorehouse from the halls of Congress to have them send someone over and diaper you, but you have to admit it's original.

You have to give him points for that. Creativity, I mean. Otherwise, the guy's kind of a waste of space.

WHAT I THINK ABOUT GUNS

JANE SMILEY, POSTED 4.16.2007

Some years ago, I was talking to a man about guns. At the time, I didn't really know anyone with guns (still don't), but he did. He had had guns himself. He said, "I gave my gun away, because when I had it, every time something happened that made me mad, my mind would start circling around that gun, and I would be thinking about using it. So I got rid of it and I'm glad I did." Right up front I will say that I am opposed to casual gun owner-ship, but I also realize that Americans will always have guns. Pe-riod. It's a national fetish. But the mental state my interlocutor was describing years ago is the price we have to pay, along with, of course, the accidental deaths of children and other unprepared and careless people who happen to be in the wrong place at the wrong time and in proximity to the wrong gun. What I would like is for the gun-toting right wing to admit that there is a price we pay, that senseless accidental deaths and traumas are a national cost and that it's not so clear that it's worth it, but hey, we pay it anyway because so many guns are in the hands of so many people that there would never be any getting rid of them. I would like the right wing to admit that guns are not "good" and that the right to bear arms is not an absolute virtue and that the deaths in the U.S. caused by guns are at least as problematic, philosophically, as abortion. But I'm not holding my breath.

OBABA CRACKS MY TV IN HALF

ADAM MCKAY, POSTED 3.18.2008

It didn't make sense. A politician responding to a TV news scandal during an election and he's not on the attack or the defensive. Instead he's asking us to look at the forces that shape our feelings on race and understand them. My first reaction was to call DirecTV. Clearly my antenna was out of alignment and picking up old broadcasts of *The Outer Limits* or *Playhouse 90* that are bouncing back to earth from Jupiter. Or maybe that California roll I ate was a week old and I'm unconscious on my living room floor and chemicals in my brain are sloshing towards the wish fulfillment part of my frontal lobe.

But it happened. Barack Obama spoke like an enlightened leader from 2008 instead of like the fake cowboy from 1885 that most politicians evoke or like a pharmaceutical salesman talking about change, but "not that much change" at a team building exercise in Tahoe. In other words, he didn't pass the buck to save his own ass. It was a monumental moment in modern American politics. He didn't distract, deflect, or attempt to frighten. He didn't accuse, declare war, or get angry. He didn't game play, scapegoat, or blame. Can you imagine? We need to engrave this shit onto a commemorative coin, fast.

Corporate tabloid news coverage, the influence of lobbyists and opinion polls have turned our politicians into the biggest group of hacks since the writing staff for *Real People* disbanded in the eighties. It's been all button pushing and gamesmanship for our representatives over the past twenty years. Anyone who stepped out of line (Howard Dean, Jimmy Carter, Paul Wellstone) was either written off as boring, naive, or nuts. All real issues faded to the background and instead "gay marriage" and "tax breaks" and "military photo ops" became the go-to bag of hack political tricks. And our newspapers and TV news shows loved it because it took the discussion away from anything constructive and instead veered it towards juicy programming (Governor is Gay! Congressman involved in Three-way! Do Gay Flag Burners Want to Pick Up Your Kids on the Internet?! etc.) and the corporate agenda.

But today's speech was different.

 ## ROMNEY & ME
LAWRENCE O'DONNELL JR., POSTED 12.13.2007

After the *Today* show used video clips of me talking (ranting, to some) about the racist history of the Church of Latter Day Saints as a lead-in to Matt Lauer's interview of Mitt Romney, I feel compelled to clarify the obvious: Religious affiliation is not a good reason to vote for or against a candidate for president. I mean any religious affiliation, including Scientology (if that's a religion). I know at least one Scientologist who would be a better president than many of the current candidates. I might know more, but they tend to be a bit secretive about being Scientologists, so . . .

I don't hate Mormons. Some of my best friends are Mormons. Well, okay, one of my best friends is Mormon. Or used to be. He's not sure anymore. He's glad he grew up Mormon, likes the values he learned, the respect for family, etc. He's just not sure about some of the crazy beliefs of the religion. He would like to distance himself from some of that stuff and still be a Mormon—the way Rudy Giuliani can be pro-abortion and very fond of divorce and sequential marriage and still be, or at least call himself, a Catholic. But Mormonism isn't as flexible as Catholicism. It's a hook, line and sinker deal. You buy it all—every word of the Book of

Mormon and its supplement, the Book of Abraham—or you're not a Mormon. My friend is a surgeon. He says the Mormon doctors he knows are like him. They have doubts about some things in the books and there are some things in the books that they simply can no longer believe. He can't imagine any Mormon who graduates from medical school or Harvard Business School like Mitt Romney thinking any other way. But if Romney were to admit to such doubts and reservations, the Church of Latter Day Saints would be forced to say he is no longer a Mormon. And a candidate for president without a religion . . . well, that could only happen on *The West Wing*.

 ## FISA IS RATINGS POISON
MARTY KAPLAN, POSTED 2.15.2008

Friday morning, President Bush came out of a meeting with Republican congressional leaders and blasted House Democrats for not performing precisely the kind of fellatio on his FISA bill that he had requested. His statement was designed to get Democrats-are-soft-on-terror into the news cycle as he headed off on Air Force 1 to Africa. It worked: the cable nets covered it live. And then, CNN cut away to DeKalb, Illinois, where, we were told, "CNN correspondents have fanned out" to explore every conceivable aspect of the tragedy of the shooter-suicide.

Imagine if, instead, after Bush's statement, we were told that CNN correspondents had fanned out to cover every aspect of the FISA impasse. Instead of feeding us eye-witness accounts of the lone gunman, we would have heard firsthand accounts of telecom employees ordered to give spy agencies total electronic access to all Americans' communications with one another. Instead of offering color about a quiet campus struck by tragedy, imagine if cable news had provided a timely explanation of the FISA law we already have, with its existing provisions for wiretaps with judicial review. Instead of reporters asking why this black-clad, deranged student could have done such a terrible lawless thing, we would have had reporters asking why companies that caved under lawless government pressure should now be retroactively pardoned for their cravenness.

Yeah, I know why it doesn't go down like that. FISA is old; DEATH IN ILLINOIS is new.

 ## HILLARY THE ADMONISHER

NORA EPHRON, POSTED 8.27.2008

My favorite part of Hillary Clinton's speech last night was when she admonished her followers not to put their affection for her over the issues. When she reminded them that what's at stake is far more crucial than their loyalty to her. When she reproved them for thinking for even a moment that her historic, thrilling campaign was more important than the real campaign to defeat the Republicans.

Where any of her followers could have gotten the idea doesn't seem to have crossed her mind. The fish stinks from the head down. The Clintons' narcissism (and yes, I know, it's an overused term but if there was ever a moment for it in our national life, this is it) perfumed every bit of Hillary's campaign, and it leaked down to her contributors and followers. "Were you in it for me?" was her funniest line of the night.

In this morning's *Times* there's a piece about the Hillraisers, the people who raised over $300,000 for Hillary, many of whom are apparently bitter and angry that they were not given rooms in the Denver Ritz-Carlton, as the early Obama fundraisers were. They are so mad, according to the *Times*, that some of them are flying home today and deliberately missing Obama's speech on Thursday. (If you're not nice to me I'm just going to take my private plane and go home.) These are people who, may I remind you, were thinking about their Cabinet and sub-Cabinet positions, who were dreaming of ambassadorships, who were on the verge of looking at houses in Georgetown. They're miserable. They lost. They were wrong. They're worth millions, or in some cases, billions, and they're not used to being wrong, much less to paying a price for being wrong, and they can't stand it. There's an expression for this—narcissistic mortification—and you can smell it all the way from Denver.

 ## SENATOR MCCAIN ISN'T FUNNY, SO STOP ENCOURAGING HIM

BOB CESCA, POSTED 7.17.2008

Last week, in response to a serious question about Iran, the Republican presumptive nominee joked about killing Iranians with weaponized cancer. This week, it's news about a joke involving gorillas and rape:

"Did you hear the one about the woman who is attacked on the street by a gorilla, beaten senseless, raped repeatedly, and left to die? When she finally regains consciousness and tries to speak, her doctor leans over to hear her sigh contently and to feebly ask, 'Where is that marvelous ape?' "

Get it? Women like to be beaten and raped. Hoo-hoo! In days past, it's been jokes about wife-beating, bombing Iran, Chelsea Clinton's looks, and Alzheimer's disease. Based on these precedents, I can only imagine Senator McCain's forthcoming zingers about still-births, burn victims, and Thalidomide.

But not unlike the president's overly jocular behavior during serious questions or serious crisis, for Senator McCain it's all about context and tone. How should a president behave in public? No one expects the presidency to be monastical, of course. In fact, many of our greatest presidents were able to use comedy to their advantage, and more than a few of them knew how to make with the profanity. But, like anything, there's a time and place for such behavior. There's a context.

The president isn't you and me. You and I can tell whatever joke we want whenever we want because we don't have to represent 300 million people on the world stage. Your personal behavior doesn't necessarily get passed on to posterity as a reflection of an entire era in American history. So if you want to tell that gorilla rape joke to your spouse or parents, have at it. If Senator McCain wants to tell a joke like that, he embarrasses more than just himself.

 ## NEW ORLEANS: NOBODY ASKED, WHY NOT SOONER?

HARRY SHEARER, POSTED 8.30.2008

The hope is that Hurricane Gustav doesn't prove the fragile repairs of the deeply defective levee and floodwall system in New Orleans have been repairs in name only, that the storm goes west, or east, that it peters out, or, most miraculously, that the repairs by the Army Corps of Engineers actually strengthened the system to a point where it can protect the city.

But one question does need to be raised now, before we know next week's outcome. After Katrina, the Corps wasted nine months in lying and refuting the findings of expert teams of engineers—the Corps insisted the levees were over-topped, while the teams reported disturbing evidence of construction and design flaws. Finally, after denigrating the experts for months, calling them liars in the local press, the Corps issued its own report in June 2006, calling the system it had designed and constructed "a system in name only."

Most crucially, the Corps announced that the system would be repaired, up to the advertised level of the pre-K system, the so-called 100-year storm, by 2011.

Maybe somebody in Congress asked, in some hearing, Why will this take six years? But nobody asked that question in public, nor the obvious followup: What's the city, and its citizens, supposed to do in the meantime, say, in 2008?

The old slogan, in engineering as in many other lines of work, is that you can have it good, fast, and cheap—pick two out of three. Is money the reason New Orleans has to wait three more years before even the semblance of protection is in place? If so, what politician, Democratic or Republican, will speak up to suggest that that schedule needs to be accelerated, that good and fast has to replace good and cheap?

 ## THE 82ND AIRBORNE VS. THE BROOKINGS INSTITUTION: WHO DO YOU TRUST FOR A REAL VIEW OF IRAQ?

PAUL RIECKHOFF, POSTED 8.20.2007

Bottom line: No scholarly articles can replace real boots-on-the-ground knowledge. Participating in a heavily secured, carefully orchestrated sight-seeing visit to Iraq does not make you a military expert any more than a trip to Yankee stadium qualifies one to be a baseball broadcaster for ESPN. That should be obvious by now.

But the media continually treats troops as wallpaper footage to run in the background while the latest talking-head pseudo-expert pontificates. And the White House hasn't learned the lesson, either, judging by the so-called "Petraeus report" coming out in September. The White House announced last week that this report won't actually be written by General Petraeus. Once again experienced military leaders will be overruled by air-conditioned bureaucrats and Beltway experts.

So let's call the Petraeus Report what it is: Yet Another White House Plan. Of course, those don't have a great track record, especially when it comes to assessing the situation on the ground. In the meantime, as more Americans and Iraqi civilians die waiting for someone in power to listen to the troops on the ground, someone should call the Brookings Institution—I can think of seven sharp 82nd Airborne soldiers who are getting back from Iraq soon, and they could use some comfy think-tank fellowships.

 ## HOW MUCH DID MCCAIN PAY FOR THE HILLARY HANDBOOK?

TREY ELLIS, POSTED 7.28.2008

It really seems that the only voting bloc McCain is courting these days is that of the Angry Old Man.

Not since the NAACP convention has McCain made a single non-vituperative comment about Obama. Instead, McCain's answer to "Yes, we can," seems to be "HEY YOU KIDS. GET THE HELL OFF MY LAWN!"

Before this campaign I always had a bit of a soft spot for McCain, the lone Republican to stand up to the Bush disaster. Two years ago I assumed the two nominees would have been McCain and Hillary and although I would have voted for Hillary, I didn't really think there would be that big of a difference.

Well, that well of goodwill has long since dried up. Much has been made of McCain's scurrilous contention that Obama is a traitor who would rather lose the war than a political contest, but it was McCain's reptilian smile after delivering the line that sent a chill down my spine. I've seen him charming and light on *The Daily Show* but it really seems that the main substance flowing through his veins these days is hate. How else to explain the ad his camp is running now saying Obama would rather play basketball than visit wounded troops? If that came from some rich rightwing nut I would have just shrugged it off, but to hear "I'm John McCain and I approve this message" at the end was a shock. When George Bush and Karl Rove spread the rumor that McCain had an illegitimate black baby they at least had the good sense to cover their asses with plausible deniability.

 ## SAY WHAT YOU WILL (REQUIEM FOR A TV NEWS CAREER)

CHEZ PAZIENZA, POSTED 2.18.2008

When I got into television, I did my best to bury my inner revolutionary. For sixteen years I've been a successful producer and manager of TV news, cranking out creative, occasionally daring content on good days and solid, no-frills material on the days in-between. I've won several awards and for the most part can say that I'm proud of what I've done in the business, particularly since I never intended to get into it in the first place; by the time college was over, I was playing steadily in a band and fully believed sleeping on floors and subsisting on beer and Taco Bell to be an entirely noble endeavor. I wound up working at WSVN in Miami only after the band imploded, taking my dreams of rock 'n' roll glory with it. Since those earliest days, I've come to understand that the libertine, pirate-ship mentality I found so seductive during my time in a rock band is pretty much a staple of most newsrooms, particularly at the local level. What's more, it's accompanied by a slightly better paycheck (although often only slightly).

Over the past several years though, something has changed. Drastically. And I'm not sure whether it's me, or television news, or both.

With the exception of the period immediately following 9/11, which saw the best characteristics of television journalism shocked back into focus and the passion of even the most jaded and cynical of its practitioners return like a shot of adrenaline to the heart, the profession I once loved and felt honored to be a part of has lost its way.

I say this with the knowledge of implied complicity: I continued to draw a salary from stations at the local level and national networks long after I had noticed an unsettling trend in which real news was being regularly abandoned in favor of, well, crap. I may not have drank the Kool-Aid, but I did take the money. I may have been uncomfortable with a lot of what I was putting on the air, but I was comfortable in the life that it provided me. I just figured, screw it, most people don't like their jobs; shut up and do what you're told, or at least try to. Besides, I told myself, what the hell else do you know how to do?

That attitude began to change in April of 2006—when I found out that I had a tumor the size of a pinball inside my head.

I was working for CNN at the time, a job I had been proud to accept three years earlier, as CNN was in my mind the gold standard of television journalism. I readily admit that it was Time Warner's medical plan that provided me the best care possible for the removal of the tumor and during my subsequent recovery, but following my operation, what had been clawing at my insides for years finally began to come to the surface. TV news wasn't the least bit fulfilling anymore, and I either needed to get out of it once and for all or find an outlet for my nascent iconoclastic tendencies.

So I started a blog.

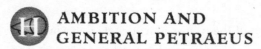

AMBITION AND GENERAL PETRAEUS

DAVID BROMWICH, POSTED 9.7.2007

Ambition is a peculiar thing. When you see the footage of General Petraeus striding with his army guard in Baghdad, sharing with reporters his familiar knowledge of the facts on the ground, ordering walls to be built and protection given for the right part of the populace and calling in air strikes to wipe out the wrong part— you are seeing a man in his element. He loves this command. It suits his life-preparation as nothing else could do; it rounds out, with practice, the theory he codified in his manual on guerrilla wars. But he is living a contradiction. His manual made it clear that a mission of this scope could never succeed without far more troops than the U.S. can hope to supply.

None of the contradictions matter to Petraeus. He cannot afford to let them matter. But a different sense of reality should prevail among the senators, even as they listen to him politely. And let them not for a moment forget who he is (since he himself will hardly forget). He is the man the president chose for the public to believe in, now that they are done believing in George W. Bush.

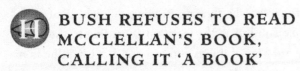 BUSH REFUSES TO READ MCCLELLAN'S BOOK, CALLING IT 'A BOOK'

ANDY BOROWITZ, POSTED 5.28.2008

On a day when Washington was abuzz with the news that former White House spokesperson Scott McClellan had published a tell-all memoir, President George W. Bush offered his personal reason for not reading it.

"I have no intention of reading Scott McClellan's book," Mr. Bush told reporters, "because it's a book."

Mr. Bush said he was "surprised" that Mr. McClellan had written a book to criticize him because "if you're trying to communicate some criticism to me, a book is pretty much the last place you'd put it."

The president said that he thought the chances of his someday reading Mr. McClellan's book were "zero," adding, "If I didn't read the Iraq Study Group's report, I really don't think I'm about to read Scott McClellan's little book."

Presidential historian Davis Logsdon of the University of Minnesota observed that if Mr. McClellan honestly expected his memoir to somehow reach Mr. Bush's nightstand, "that demonstrates just how little he knows George W. Bush.

"Scott McClellan would have had a much better shot if he had put his memoir in Xbox 360 format and then slipped it into a package labeled 'Grand Theft Auto 5,' " he said.

ROSE GARDEN COLORED GLASSES

ANDY STERN, POSTED 10.25.2007

Straight from the folks who thought Brownie did "a heck of a job," we now can take comfort in the fact that according to the White House, "There are a lot of things you can say about half the families in America. Half of them aren't poor."

It's hard not interpret this as another sign of an administration that is profoundly out of touch with the lives of working people all around this country. But maybe what we've got here is a glass-half-full kind of guy celebrating his milestones where he can find them. After all—a little cockeyed optimism at the White House probably brightens some of the darker headlines these days.

So donning our Rose Garden colored glasses, here's some other good news from the Bush administration:

- More than half of all the homes in this country have not been foreclosed on—yet.
- More than half of the residents of New Orleans were not permanently displaced by Hurricane Katrina.
- More than half of Halliburton executives haven't been indicted.
- More than half of the polar ice caps are still in place.
- More than half of Americans who don't have health insurance probably won't get sick today.
- More than half of college graduates won't have to declare bankruptcy immediately because of their student loan debt.
- More than half of oil company executives can still afford to fill their cars' gas tanks.

- More than half the nations of the world still return our phone calls.

With this kind of good news, it's no surprise that well more than half of Americans are counting the days until the Bush administration is no more.

TOYOTA'S GREEN BUBBLE BURSTING?

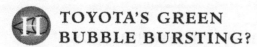

LAURIE DAVID, POSTED 10.9.2007

Toyota has gotten a lot of mileage out of portraying itself as the greenest, most fuel-efficient car company on the planet, and has reaped the benefits both financially and public relations–wise. Yet they are careening toward becoming the most hypocritical car company on the planet by aggressively opposing desperately needed higher U.S. fuel-economy standards. Toyota should be worried that their green bubble will burst.

Let's take a little stock here. The company has sold over 1 million hybrids to consumers who'd rather sip gas than guzzle it, and who want to do their part in the battle against global warming.

But now Toyota is teaming up with Detroit's Big Three to scuttle legislation that would raise fuel economy standards to 35 miles per gallon by 2020—a technologically feasible, and urgently needed step for a country President Bush has admitted is "addicted to oil." When our nation is contributing more CO_2 pollution than any other—and fueling the global climate crisis—isn't it the reasonable thing to do to perhaps, I don't know, become more efficient?

For those customers who bought the Prius long before it was "cool" and thought they were investing in Toyota's vision of a gas-sipping fleet, this latest move is insulting. It's a slap in the face to every driver who has helped make Toyota the first foreign company to surpass all the American car companies in sales. We believed the company when it said it was a leader, that it had a vision to sell a million hybrids a year and make its fleet 100 percent hybrid, that it wanted to help move America beyond our addiction to oil. And now this?

WGA STRIKE: HOW THINGS HAVE CHANGED

ALEC BALDWIN, POSTED 12.24.2007

Speculation about the WGA strike, when it will end and how, seems like such a waste. An understandable one, but a waste nonetheless. What's important is understanding how things have changed.

Corporations that once controlled so much of the movie, television, and record industries could afford to lavish their talent, craftspeople, and themselves with generous, if not mind-boggling, compensation. When three networks called all of the shots, when movies were made with more of an eye toward content than marketing, when popular music uplifted the soul rather than deadened it, it seemed that everyone was paid a lot of money, from the grips to the drivers to the stars to the studio heads.

However, when Bruce Willis was paid $5 million for a movie, things began to change. We entered a period wherein everyone wanted, and got, more. You knew that things were distorted when agents started getting rich. Not the owners of the agencies, not the Norman Brokaws on the scene. Regular Ten Percenters began making seven figures. That was a big change. Once agents saw salaries rise and their own income potential with it, the old-school practices of developing clients began to die. If you want to get repped by a good agency today, you have to walk in the door printing money.

 ## LET BUSH BE REAGAN

BILL MAHER, POSTED 9.27.2007

For the next eighteen months, let Bush be Reagan. A completely dissociative personality who lets the real work of the nation go on elsewhere, while he sits behind his desk and hums. I don't think the problem is that Bush lives in a bubble. I say make the bubble thicker. Use the armor we can't get to the troops. For example, on this whole "bomb Iran" thing. Let's not, and just tell him we did.

Who's going to tell him the truth? Rove? Gonzales? Rummy? Scooter? Harriet Miers? It's like a haunted house. The douchebag cupboard is bare.

According to *The Times* of London, the Air Force has drawn up plans for massive strikes against 1,200 targets in Iran. The plan doesn't just call for eliminating Iran's nuclear program, but for taking out its entire military in one blow. Can Bush destroy another country's whole army? Why not? He did it to ours.

We'll get Condi to slip him a note. "Mr. President, Iran is free!" And he'll scribble some garbled bullshit on it, like "Let freedom Purple Rain" and that will be that.

Mission Accomplished. Oh, and the astronauts you sent to Mars just called. They said to say "hi."

He'll never know. According to a classified report on White House crowd management, protesters are not only kept out of Bush's sight at rallies, they must be kept where he can't see them from his car. Frat boys are recruited to chant "USA! USA!" over hecklers. Bush has also been told that your approval rating is like your golf score, and the asshole with the lowest one wins.

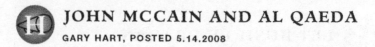

JOHN MCCAIN AND AL QAEDA
GARY HART, POSTED 5.14.2008

Historians of early 21st century American politics will remark the degree to which radical forces, usually called neoconservatives, perverted language as recommended by the National Socialist Party in 1930s Germany. Continue to demonize liberals, blame them for all social and economic problems, and soon enough no one will be willing to admit to being a liberal. Claim that liberals and Democrats are too soft to combat terrorists and soon enough a majority, even in the oldest democracy on earth, will believe it. Open up entire electronic networks, such as Fox, and chains of radio stations, such as Clear Channel, and buy enough newspaper chains, and make all these media available to pre-programmed neoconservative ditto heads, and sure enough a subculture will emerge which distrusts its own government and believes that an entire political party is not to be trusted.

This has all happened before. And where it has happened, authoritarian government emerges.

Worst of all, a formerly "maverick" Republican, one who was sensible enough to understand the dangerous perversions involved in this radicalization of American politics, will find himself repeating the idiotic mantra that we are "fighting al Qaeda in Iraq so we don't have to fight them here."

John McCain knows better. I know he knows better. But it is appalling when a serious patriot like McCain is forced to fall into line with these radical perverters of language, one of the most dangerous things that can happen in a democracy, in order to lead a party that is so far off the mainstream rails that it will take decades to return to civility and normality.

If John McCain seriously believes we are at war with al Qaeda in Iraq, that alone is such a serious error in judgment as to rank him with George W. Bush at his worst and therefore disqualify him from any chance to govern this country.

 ## THE SUICIDE SOLUTION

BARBARA EHRENREICH, POSTED 7.28.2008

Suicide is becoming an increasingly popular response to debt. James Scurlock's brilliant documentary, *Maxed Out*, features the families of two college students who killed themselves after being overwhelmed by credit card debt. "All the people we talked to had considered suicide at least once," Scurlock told a gathering of the National Association of Consumer Bankruptcy Attorneys in 2007. According to the *Los Angeles Times*, lawyers in the audience backed him up, "describing clients who showed up at their offices with cyanide, or threatened, 'If you don't help me, I've got a gun in my car.'"

India may be the trendsetter here, with an estimated 150,000 debt-ridden farmers succumbing to suicide since 1997. With guns in short supply in rural India, the desperate farmers have taken to drinking the pesticides meant for their crops.

Dry your eyes, already: Death is an effective remedy for debt, along with anything else that may be bothering you too. And try to think of it too from a lofty, corner-office, perspective: If you can't pay your debts or afford to play your role as a consumer, and if, in addition—like an ever-rising number of Americans—you're no longer needed at the workplace, then there's no further point to your existence. I'm not saying that the creditors, the bankers, and the mortgage companies actually want you dead, but in a culture where one's credit rating is routinely held up as a three-digit measure of personal self-worth, the correct response to insoluble debt is in fact, "Just shoot me!"

The alternative is to value yourself more than any amount of money and turn the guns, metaphorically speaking, in the other direction. It wasn't God, or some abstract economic climate change, that caused the credit crisis. Actual humans—often masked as financial institutions—did that, (and you can find a convenient list of names in Nomi Prins's article in the current issue of *Mother Jones.*) Most of them, except for a tiny few facing trials, are still high rollers, fattening themselves on the blood and tears of ordinary debtors. I know it's so 1930s, but may I suggest a march on Wall Street?

 RIDING IN A FIGHTER PLANE AND GETTING SHOT DOWN AND WHAT IT QUALIFIES YOU FOR

DAVID REES, POSTED 7.2.2008

Let's review:

Bob Schieffer of *Face the Nation* made an important point: Unlike all-American war hero John McCain, Barack Obama has never "ridden in a fighter plane and gotten shot down."

In response, General Wesley Clark (traitor) said that riding in a fighter plane and getting shot down. . . doesn't actually qualify a person to be president.

And then everyone on TV exploded.

How DARE left-wing pacifist Wesley Clark suggest that riding in a fighter plane and getting shot down doesn't automatically qualify someone to be president?

Riding in a fighter plane and getting shot down automatically qualifies you to be anything.

(Except a good fighter pilot.)

Let's review:

Riding in a fighter plane and getting shot down: AUTOMATI-CALLY QUALIFIES YOU TO BE PRESIDENT.

Riding on a city bus and running off a bridge: QUALIFIES YOU TO BE VICE-PRESIDENT.

Riding on a rollercoaster and flying out of your seat but then landing on a waterslide and sliding down to into the water and almost drowning but then being rescued by an Elvis imperson-ator: QUALIFIES YOU TO BE SECRETARY OF THE INTE-RIOR.

Getting your foot run over by a fire truck: QUALIFIES YOU TO BE COMMISSIONER OF THE FDA.

Riding on a unicycle while eating a bran muffin: QUALIFIES YOU TO BE POET LAUREATE.

Falling off a really, really tall ladder and being captured by lawn gnomes and taken to their underground lair (behind the azaleas) and being tortured for five years by their evil, tiny ceramic hands: QUALIFIES YOU TO BE DEPUTY SECRETARY OF DE-FENSE FOR LANDSCAPING.

Getting really, really drunk at Thanksgiving and crying, "Why was I never good enough for you, Dad?" and then literally eating a banjo, and then saying, "Am I man enough NOW, Dad? Now that I've eaten my banjo—the one thing I loved, the one thing you could never understand?": QUALIFIES YOU TO BE CHAIR-MAN OF THE FEDERAL RESERVE.

Riding on one of those old-timey bicycles with the gigantic front wheel and wearing a handlebar mustache and saying, "By Jove, isn't everything wonderful here in olden tymes, I wonder what amusement is to be had at the nickel-theatre": QUALIFIES YOU TO BE BOB SCHIEFFER.

I AM NOT GAY

HILARY ROSEN, POSTED 8.28.2007

Larry Craig isn't gay. Thank god cuz we don't really want him to be. Ick. Now that he has told the country that he isn't gay in a press conference, I am so relieved.

I don't want him to be gay because he is such a pathetic figure. Bearing his outrage but not his shame before the cameras today. Fine, Senator. Don't be gay. There are lots of people who don't identify as gay but DO have sex with guys (or women) sometimes. But those people usually don't have the power to pursue discriminatory laws against gays and lesbians or promote hostile viewpoints against us in the halls of Congress. We all have enough information about how hypocritical it would be if someone like Senator Craig were to actually BE gay and vote in such an anti-gay manner. I won't bother making that point since I frankly don't think voting to hurt people is justified no matter what your sexual orientation.

Ironically on the LGBT blogs and "insider lists" today there was a huge discussion about whether or not Senator Craig should garner some sympathy from the community because of the historic antipathy that exists towards police entrapment methods against, particularly, gay men.

But seeing his performance, I have lost any notion of sympathy. The guy practically SPIT it out that he wasn't gay. Because if he WAS gay, then that would somehow explain his publicly lewd behavior.

Like I said, ick.

THE UNBEARABLE LIGHTNESS OF BEING KARL ROVE

JAMES MOORE, POSTED 6.25.2008

Instead of being vilified for what he has done to his country, his party, and his president, Rove finds doors open to him down every hall he walks. The media, which he often had the president refer to as "the filter," is embracing his intellectual dishonesty with both money and fervor. Never mind that Rove hasn't spent an adult day of his life without spitting out the words "reporter" or "media" as though they were so much risen bile. He is now one of the people he had long positioned as an enemy. He writes for *Newsweek* and *The Wall Street Journal,* opines on Fox News, and in his spare moments gives speeches at $60,000 a pop while also working on his memoir, which fetched a $1.2 million advance.

Of course, he isn't exactly laboring for media outlets that are without bias. Rove makes no pretense to either objectivity or fairness. His task is to frame everything up to raise doubt about Democrats and rewrite the failures of his president and his party. The questions to be asked aren't as much about Rove as they are about why any part of our culture still takes him seriously.

SURVEYING THE
REPUBLICAN FIELD

JERRY AND JOE LONG, POSTED 1.24.2008

MITT ROMNEY

All you have to do to know that Romney is a prick is look at him. It requires a certain kind of transcendent scumbagness to take genuine offense when your own words are quoted back to you.

Yet it's not nearly as troubling to hear The Gelled Hedge Funder babble on about the great good greatness of our shining hills and seas as it is to think of the collective IQ of those for whom this constitutes a reason to support him.

Though it was quite a "Paris is worth a mass" moment to see the candidate who believes the Garden of Eden was in Missouri attempt to reassure those who believe there were dinosaurs on Noah's Ark that he shares their values.

MIKE HUCKABEE

The swingin' preacher, always ready to lay down a funky bass-line or a self-deprecating quip, has voiced some genuinely un-Republican views about the plight of the poor. Unfortunately, he has also voiced some genuinely unconstitutional views about the meaning of the Establishment Clause and some genuinely un-hinged views about the age of the earth.

RUDY GIULIANI

The original first responder, who parlayed authoritatively walking through rubble into a sleazy personal fortune.

Apparently, if he wins Florida Rudy will grab a Bible and rush to the West Front of the Capitol to swear himself in. Yet while the media is intent on focusing on the pros or cons of his strategy, shouldn't someone take a moment to ponder his maniacally brutal vindictiveness.

Tested . . . Ready . . . Now . . . hopefully refers to the involuntary commitment papers.

JOHN McCAIN

The candidate Democrats must fear to face . . . so goes the conventional wisdom. And like all conventional wisdom it fails to answer the only question that matters . . . why?

In 2000 when he was at his best, McCain's "rogue-state rollback" was an idea even Augustus would have found unworkable. Since then he has done nothing but abandon principles and kiss George Bush's ass.

So . . . a candidate whose idea of leadership is standing up to Donald Rumsfeld, who wants to stay in Iraq for a hundred years, who sees an endorsement by Joe Lieberman as a plus . . . this is someone to be feared?

Maybe . . . if the Democrats were stupid enough to nominate someone tied to the past, devoid of scruple and unfamiliar with truth, whose only absolute devotion was to maintaining power . . . but they'd never do that.

 THEY WERE WRONG

JON ROBIN BAITZ, POSTED 12.5.2007

As an amateur sinologist of Hollywood manners, I am making a pretty safe bet: that right now, the studio guys are figuring out who among them is going to get humiliated first. Because somewhere up in Parnasus, it's starting to become abundantly clear that they thought they were untouchable. And now they know: They were wrong. About too many big issues.

The studio heads thought that there was no way the writers would be able to organize themselves coherently. They were wrong. They thought the writers would be too scared to give up the rich deals, and the option payments and the easy living. They were wrong. They thought the writers didn't have the earnest and heartfelt certitude to maintain solidarity for a day, let alone five weeks. They thought that the studio machinery and the big media outlets they owned could control and get ahead of the story. And they were shocked and appalled to see how wrong they were about that. They were wrong.

They were wrong about who the writers are, and now they know it. And now we watch. Watch as the factions among the studio players start to push and pull in a quiet and volatile war for primacy. Watch as the moderates on their team, who are aware of the ticking clocks, aware of the crews who are suffering, and the cost to their industry, try to slowly wrestle the gavel away from the hard-liners. Watch as the peacemakers and diplomats continue to press for resolution, emboldened but with patience and calm, but also, with long memories. Especially if they feel they are being played.

And the peacemakers in this story are not pacifists. If you get my drift. As this week ends and an agreement is not ⌐ wouldn't look to any day in what is left of this unfortuna a resolution. The hard candy of bad-faith negotiating a amateurish pageantry from the studio side has done n further strengthen the resolve of the writers. Like my b boss and mentor, they stepped forward in contempt, an and now we watch the proverbial chickens come home think this labor action should serve to put the purveyors of mega-new media corporatism on notice that the old game, the old trope of "schmucks with Underwoods" is at this point, in the 21st century, almost entirely denuded of any truth or viability.

 ## BUSH TO KIDS: DROP DEAD!

STEVEN WEBER, POSTED 10.4.2007

"Poor kids first," the Great Dissembler said.

"I believe in private medicine, not the federal government running the health care system," Der Alte Smirker intoned.

And on the sly, he vetoed the bill that would have allotted $35 billion to a health care system from which Americans would benefit, while continuing to rubber stamp the nearly $1 trillion to fund his war-for-hire machine.

You see, by getting health care to more Americans, the government's allies in Big Pharma will feel the squeeze. And they don't like to be squeezed. Not by their mothers. And not by consumers. And after all, revamping health care to allow the majority of Americans participation in a prohibitively expensive system, in which those with mucho moolah can get the best care but those with less cabbage can't is (gasp) Socialized Medicine. It's what the Commies would have done had they won the Cold War instead of us. They would have overrun their newly conquered slaves with affordable health care, those savages. Then maybe the average life span of Americans would be up there with Cuba, Denmark, Chile, South Korea, the United Arab Emirates, Luxembourg, Costa Rica, Ireland, Cyprus, Guadeloupe, Finland, Germany, The United Kingdom, Malta, Belgium, Greece, Martinique, the Netherlands, Austria, Singapore, Norway, New Zealand, Italy, Canada, France, Macau, Israel, Sweden, Spain,

Australia, Switzerland, Iceland, Hong Kong, and Japan, most of whom have universal health care systems. And for expediency's sake, these countries are now to be referred to as The Axis of Live.

It seems Red is actually better than Dead.

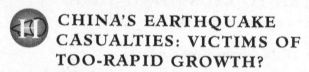

CHINA'S EARTHQUAKE CASUALTIES: VICTIMS OF TOO-RAPID GROWTH?

NATHAN GARDELS, POSTED 5.14.2008

Since the Chinese authorities seems to be practicing more glasnost with respect to the Sichuan quake than any previous natural or manmade disaster, we'll probably know the facts down the road a bit. But anyone who goes regularly to China can't but wonder whether there is a very strong link between the quickest pace of economic growth in history and buildings which go up too fast to stand the test of time and nature.

The New York Times reports this morning (May 15) that local residents of Dujiangyan, in the heart of the quake zone, are angrily calling for an investigation into why government buildings remained standing while schools didn't. One man told the *NYT* that two additional stories had been added to the Xinjian school even though it had failed a safety inspection two years ago.

Speaking about the Shenzhen Special Economic Zone near Hong Kong, which went in one decade from a fishing village of 30,000 people to a metropolis of 3.5 million, Deng Xiaoping, godfather of modern China, once praised the spirit of the place as an example for others: "Their slogan," he enthused, "is 'time is money, efficiency is livelihood.' In buildings undergoing construction, one floor is finished every day and the entire building is completed within a couple of weeks or so."

The pace of building has been so rapid over the years in Shenzhen that the Harvard Design School Project on the city in 2001 coined the phrase "Shenzhen Speed©" to signify the stunning pace of throwing up structures. The record design speeds they listed include: 5 designers $\times$ 1 night + 2 computers = 300 unit single-family housing development; 1 architect $\times$ 3 nights = 7 story walk-up apartment; 1 architect $\times$ 7 days = 30 story concrete residential high-rise.

Of course, Shenzen is a long way from Sichuan province where the earthquake is.

We all know that pollution and inequality are downsides to the truly remarkable Chinese miracle. To them we must now add, it appears, faulty structures that, for all the speed in which they are constructed, are no match for nature's jolts when geologic time strikes.

MY BROTHER THE SUPERDELEGATE AND WHY I DON'T TRUST HIM TO PICK THE NEXT PRESIDENT

ARI EMANUEL, POSTED 2.10.2008

My brother Rahm Emanuel is a superdelegate. I love my brother, and I trust my brother. But I gave up letting my brother dictate my life since he determined whether he got the top or bottom bunk in our bedroom back in Chicago.

So, as much as I love and respect him, I don't trust him and his fellow superdelegates to decide for me and the American people who should be the Democratic nominee—and, therefore, most likely the next president of the United States.

I want voters to make that decision. The superdelegates, my brother included, have not been elected by anybody to name the nominee. They've either been appointed by the party or, as in my brother's case, have automatically inherited the role simply because they are elected officials. This isn't the place to debate the entire history of superdelegates. Suffice it to say, however, they were created by the party machine decades ago for the express purpose of giving party insiders the ability to thwart the popular will.

After what Democrats went through in Florida in 2000, we should be the first to reject any such funny business. We should be as opposed to superdelegates changing the course of an election as we were to the Supreme Court appointing George W. Bush president.

The right thing for my brother, and all the other superdelegates to do, is to support the decision of the voters. Whichever candidate has won the most delegates going into the national convention should be granted the endorsement of the superdelegates. Period.

THE OLYMPICS AND CHINESE SOFT POWER

JOSEPH NYE, POSTED 8.24.2008

"Soft power" has now entered China's official language. In his keynote speech to the 17th National Congress of the Communist Party of China (CPC) on October 15, 2007, Hu Jintao stated that the CPC must "enhance culture as part of the soft power of our country to better guarantee the people's basic cultural rights and interests."

China has always had an attractive traditional culture, but now it is entering the realm of global popular culture as well. Yao Ming, the Chinese star of the National Basketball Association's Houston Rockets, could become another Michael Jordan, and while China lost to the U.S. in basketball, Yao was one of the stars of the Beijing Olympics. The enrollment of foreign students in China has tripled from 36,000 to 110,000 over the past decade, and the number of foreign tourists has also increased dramatically to 17 million per year even before the Olympics. In addition, China has created some two hundred Confucius Institutes around the world to teach its language and culture, and while the Voice of America's was cutting its Chinese broadcasts from nineteen to fourteen hours a day, China Radio International was increasing its broadcasts in English to twenty-four hours a day.

But just as China's economic and military power does not yet match that of the United States, China's soft power still has a long way to go. China does not have cultural industries like Hollywood, and its universities are not yet the equal of America's. It lacks the many non-governmental organizations that generate much of America's soft power. Politically, China suffers from corruption, inequality, and a lack of democracy, human rights, and the rule of law. While that may make Beijing attractive in authoritarian and semi-authoritarian developing countries, it undercuts China's soft power in the West. Given the domestic problems that China must still overcome, there are limits to China's ability to attract others, but one would be foolish to ignore the gains it is making. The Beijing Olympics were an important part of China's strategy to increase its soft power.

MORALS TO BE DRAWN FROM SPITZER'S 'CASE'

ERICA JONG, POSTED 3.11.2008

1. Pay hookers in cash.
2. Think globally, act locally: Don't cross state lines to get laid.
3. Don't use "George Fox" as a pseudonym.
4. If using a pseudonym, make up a phony address. Revealing the marital residence on Fifth Avenue is a bad idea.
5. Don't try to avoid using condoms with women named Kristen.
6. Never send cash by mail.
7. Be skeptical about institutions with sexist names like The Emperor's Club.
8. Don't yell at investment bankers on the phone.
9. If you are famous for closing prostitution rings, don't frequent them.
10. While in public office, fuck your own wife—unless you are in French politics.

ACKNOWLEDGMENTS

For starters, we want to thank the over two thousand bloggers whose consistently engaging work has made it possible for Huff-Post's editors to be in a position to write a book about blogging—with a special hat tip to those HuffPosters who offered their anecdotes, insights, and advice to include in our book.

Thanks to Simon & Schuster publisher David Rosenthal for his support and encouragement—and for approaching us with the idea. That idea would never have become a book without Aileen Boyle, our wonderful editor. Her expertise and perseverance were essential in making this project happen.

Much gratitude to the rest of the Simon & Schuster team: Irene Kheradi and Michael Szczerban in managing editorial, art director Michael Accordino, marketing manager Leah Wasielewski, legal counsel Elisa Rivlin, publicity mavens Victoria Meyer and Katie Grinch, copy editor Jonathan Evans, interior designer Nancy Singer, editorial assistant Dan Cabrera, and the digital division's Ellie Hirschorn and Adrian Norman.

Leading the HuffPost charge, as always, were our cofounders,

Arianna and Ken. Simply put, without them there'd be no Huff-Post—and no HuffPost *Complete Guide to Blogging*.

Thanks to Roy Sekoff, our indefatigable HuffPost editor, who somehow always found the time (how did you find the time?) to do whatever was needed to help bring this project to completion.

Big thanks—and a blogging merit badge—to Nicholas Sabloff and Laura Vanderkam for spearheading the editorial shaping of this guide. Their resourcefulness was matched only by their dedication.

The same can be said for the hardworking members of the HuffPost blog team: senior blog editor Colin Sterling and associate blog editors David Flumenbaum, Katherine Goldstein, and Whitney Snyder.

And last, but not least, we want to thank all the members of the Huffington Post team. This is a book about blogging, but that is only one element of what has made HuffPost a destination—if not an obsession—for millions.

Please go to HuffPost's About Us section for all their names and titles. And while you're on the site, take a look around and you'll see the fruits of their labor.